THE CONSOLATIONS OF PHILOSOPHY

For Bill Lyons,

Professor of Moral Philosophy, TCD, 1985-204

Edited by Paul O'Grady

The Consolations of Philosophy:

REFLECTIONS FOR AN ECONOMIC DOWNTURN

the columba press

First edition, 2011, published by
the columba press
55A Spruce Avenue, Stillorgan Industrial Park,
Blackrock, Co Dublin

Cover by Bill Bolger
Origination by The Columba Press
Printed in Ireland by
Colour Books Ltd, Dublin

ISBN 978 1 85607 713 2

Contents

INTRODUCTION

Philosophy and Irish Culture

Paul O'Grady

A Literary Culture

There have been many significant Irish philosophers. The best known is probably George Berkeley (1685-1753), fellow of Trinity College Dublin and Bishop of Cloyne, whose philosophical works are studied by every undergraduate philosophy student. There is also John Scottus Eriugena (c. 815-877), the most important philosopher writing between the sixth and late eleventh century, as well as other figures such as John Toland (1670-1722), William Molyneux (1656-1698) and Luke Wadding (1588-1657). Nowadays there is a thriving academic philosophical culture within the Irish universities, as well as numerous distinguished Irish philosophers working abroad. Yet philosophy doesn't enter into the public discourse to any great extent in modern Ireland. The educated public is much more familiar with, for example, Yeats, Joyce and Beckett than with philosophers, Irish or otherwise. Books of history, novels, drama and poetry are more mainstream than books of philosophy.

However, the three literary figures just cited owe a great deal to philosophy and fed their literary imaginations with distinctive kinds of philosophy. Yeats saw himself as part of an Irish Protestant tradition which counted Berkeley as a major member, and he also immersed himself in the works of Plato, Plotinus, the Indian *Upanishads* and theosophy, drawing on philosophers who emphasised the spiritual dimensions of human existence. Joyce encountered Aristotle and Aquinas in his Jesuit education and the character of Stephen Daedelus works on a theory of aesthetics in *Portrait of the Artist as a Young Man*. The older Joyce used the theories of Vico on time to help structure *Finnegan's Wake*. Beckett delighted in philosophical problems and was especially interested in questions about knowledge and skepticism from the 17th century, particularly the work of Descartes and a lesser known Cartesian, Guelincx. Many of his characters inhabit a world where they struggle to escape from a solitary consciousness and make contact with something outside. Others search for meaning in a meaningless landscape, and Beckett is often associated with the French Existentialists, with whom he socialised in mid-20th-century Paris. In each of these cases, the artist has drawn on distinctive ways of looking at the world, modes of experience and kinds of sensibility in the philosophical literature, which left a clear stamp on the character of their own work.

For a very long period, the main influence on worldview and value in Irish culture has been the Catholic Church. Christianity has had a long and complex relationship with philosophy. The German philosopher Nietzsche called Christianity Platonism for the masses and there is a certain level of truth in that claim. Many of the distinctive views associated with Christian religious belief are shared with philosophical Platonism; for example that what is most real and valuable is non-material, that the soul is separate from and superior to the body, that there is an afterlife of reward or punishment, that values exist absolutely and so on. Yet just as the story of the relationship of philosophy to religious belief is not linear and simple, neither has the role of the church in Ireland been simple. The early Celtic church exhibited a high level of independence from Rome. The arrival of European religious orders with the Normans helped the process of emphasising the adjective in Roman Catholicism, but nevertheless some of them became more Irish than the Irish themselves. The Reformation clearly left its mark on Irish history and geography. Not least among the results of this was the founding of Trinity College by Elizabeth I in 1592 to spread 'proper' religion among the Irish. A century later it was a significant centre for philosophical research, with a circle of scholars gathered around Archbishop King. The Waterford-born Franciscan, Luke Wadding, in the seventeenth century, was the editor of Duns Scotus's works and a well-known European intellectual. The political pressures both within and without Ireland led to a strong conservative cast in the kind of Catholicism found in the nineteenth and twentieth century, antagonistic to other religious traditions and to the secular world. The tight interweaving of Irish public life and Catholic ideals probably reached its strongest manifestation, ironically, just as it was about to change, in 1979, with the visit of Pope John Paul II.

In the thirty-odd intervening years since then, Irish society has changed dramatically and the role of the Catholic Church with it. The sequence of referenda fought in the 1980s for the liberalisation of the constitution showed clear battle lines between a younger, urban, liberal and an older, rural, conservative, Ireland. If the forces of secularism and consumerism assailed it from without, by the time of the new millennium Irish Catholicism was beginning to implode. Various clerical scandals preceded the truly appalling revelations of clerical child sexual abuse and the institutional cover-up perpetrated by senior members of the hierarchy. It seemed as if preserving the structures was more important than acting on the actual values espoused by those structures. The moral authority of the institutional church was deeply compromised, at a time when other social institutions such as banks and politicians had lost the trust of large sections of the population.

Other strands have fed into the deep changes in Irish society. New kinds of issues and problems face us, undreamt of by earlier generations. We face massive climate change – what is the proper response? Our technologies allow us options hitherto unavailable – genetic engineering, reproductive technology, the communications explosion and the shrinking world. What principles do we use to judge what is right? What technical advances ought we limit or reject? We also now welcome a multiplicity of cultures and races into what had been a largely monocultural environment. How do we negotiate with Africans, Asians, Eastern Europeans, with Muslims?

If simple, catechism-style answers no longer suffice to answer the deep questions raised by the changes in our society, the most recent change in our economic fortunes has led to a wake-up call in terms of our values, commitments and sense of ourselves as a society. Many commentators had voiced worry that the demise of 'traditional' values had left a vacuum replaced by consumerism and the trivialities of global celebrity culture. The Celtic Tiger years extolled the virtues of wealth and consumption. A staple of ordinary conversation had been the never-ending spiral of the housing market, with informed discussions of mortgage interest relief, tracker bonds, annual percentage rates and so on. The now rather obvious thought that it was all unsustainable was not entertained in those heady years. Returning to the simple pieties of the past doesn't seem possible, yet endorsing the trivialities of global consumerist culture isn't terribly attractive either.

The current economic downturn has sharpened our sense of questioning. A bout of collective soul-searching has now convulsed the country, as we query what went wrong, who is responsible, what did we learn, if anything? It is precisely at such times of crisis, where habitual patterns of thinking no longer suffice, that philosophy comes into its own. What it offers are tools, analyses, insight and the possibility of re-imagining our society. Paul Gauguin has a famous painting entitled 'Who are we? Where do we come from? Where are we going?' These perennial questions need fresh answers from each generation and are exactly the kind of question philosophers consider.

What Can Philosophy Offer?

The Oxford English Dictionary defines a 'consolatio' as 'a thing written to expound philosophical or religious themes as comfort for the misfortunes of life' and defines 'consolation' as 'alleviation of sorrow or mental distress'. If, as a society, we are suffering misfortune and many individuals experience sorrow or mental distress, what could philosophy offer to them? Many of the great philosophers of the past lived through periods of turmoil, offering analysis and suggesting strategies for understanding and dealing with such events. One assumption shared by most of them is that a correct understanding of whatever situation one is in is a prerequisite for finding a way out.

One of the chief concerns of philosophy has been to get a correct understanding of the deep nature of reality, the fundamental structures which hold in the world. This has been construed as raising questions even more fundamental than scientific ones. For example, is reality ultimately physical? Is everything explicable in terms of matter, or energy, or do other things exist besides? Obvious candidates for such non-physical entities include God, souls and minds, and less obvious candidates might include numbers, values or abstract entities such as 'reason' or 'truth'. Debating these issues is the job of metaphysics and it serves to clarify one's basic worldview.

What values one holds can be closely connected to the worldview one has. Believing that God exists makes it more plausible to think that there are absolute moral standards which have always existed. In the absence of such a divine lawgiver, it seems more reasonable to some to hold that values evolve, change and are shaped by society. And one might hold an intermediate view which holds that there are absolute moral values, but cultures slowly and painfully clarify them and get closer to them while never fully reaching them. Ethics is the branch of philosophy which applies reason to questions about value.

Some people despair at ever getting to stable and true beliefs about the deep nature of reality or value. They think that human knowledge is too diverse and unstable to get anywhere on these issues and point to the great level of disagreement between historical periods and cultures, and even within cultures. Such a view is called skepticism and it is a distinctive position within the branch of philosophy called epistemology, or theory of knowledge. A problem with the skeptical view is that we do actually have some knowledge (reflect on the kinds of knowledge required to even entertain the skeptical hypothesis by reading this – language acquisition, literacy, ability to grasp abstract concepts). So why does the skeptic set limits to what can be known? Such debates occur in epistemology and one of the major current debates is whether there are any truths which are universal and absolute, or whether truths are relative, cultural and contingent.

A further task for philosophers is to give an account of human existence. Are we fully material entities or is there a part of us which is spiritual? What is the relationship of reason to emotion, do we have genuine free will or are we programmed by our genes? Are our plans and designs, our belief systems and worldviews illusory or real, a fairy tale or deep truths?

It should now be obvious that philosophy has some connection to the territory religion inhabits, giving answers to questions about origin, purpose and meaning. How it differs from many religious traditions is that philosophy uses only the resources of human reasoning, not accepting any privileged status for scripture or church tradition. Some philosophers were devout religious believers, including Augustine, Aquinas, Pascal, Kant and Kierkegaard. Others were zealous atheists, including Nietzsche, Marx, Russell and Sartre. Different philosophical positions variously support or challenge religious beliefs.

In the contemporary world, science has taken on the mantle of the greatest intellectual achievement of humanind. How does philosophy relate to science? Nearly all the sciences historically began within philosophy, splitting off to become a distinct discipline when clearly delineated experimental methods became available, for example, physics, psychology and linguistics. Philosophy doesn't use observational methods, using reflection and conceptual argumentation instead. This is a controversial claim – a significant strand within philosophy called 'naturalism' argues that philosophy blends into science – philosophy is just science being self-reflective. But many hold that the distinctive methods of philosophy are those which can be exercised in an armchair. Philosophy is attuned to scientific results, but is not itself a science.

One of the ways in which it differs from science is in the bewildering multiplicity of positions held in philosophy. There is no position so bizarre that a philosopher hasn't held it. Isn't that a sign of the failure of the discipline, a collapse of method? Not necessarily. We make conceptual maps of the world for ourselves, finding ways of explaining Gauguin's questions. We judge these maps in terms of how coherent they are, how they speak to our experiences, how explanatory they are, how attractive they are, what they help us do. David Hume has claimed:

> If truth be at all within the reach of human capacity, 'tis certain it must be very deep and abstruse; and to hope we shall arrive at it without pains, while the greatest geniuses have failed

with the utmost pains, must certainly be esteemed sufficiently vain and presumptuous. (*Treatise of Human Nature* 'Introduction')

Attempting to find the truth about the fundamental questions of human existence is not a simple task and needs to be pursued in a spirit of fallibility and intellectual humility. Some of the different philosophical approaches may be closer to the truth than others, but to be able to judge this requires a sufficient exposure to a variety of such approaches.

The goal of this volume is to provide such an exposure and explore a variety of different answers to the consolatory role of philosophy. No one approach is privileged, (including the approach that thinks that philosophy actually does console!). In the next section of this introduction I would like to offer an overview of the contributions, mapping them out, as it were, to chart the multiple possible consolations which philosophy can offer.

A Rich Tapestry
The chapters reflect the choices of individual authors to the question of the consolation of philosophy, so the selections do not represent a unified perspective or programmatic outlook on the question. A diversity of views exists, although clear connections exist between the positions presented.

The opening chapter deals with Boethius, who is the figure most associated with the expression 'the consolation of philosophy', the title of his great book. Paul O'Grady discusses the motivation for that work, situating Boethius in his historical and intellectual conext. Boethius offers a religious view of reality and argues that true consolation is to be found in realising the truth of that picture. He tackles deep problems which have been pitted against belief in God since antiquity. Firstly, how can one say that God exists since the world might have come to be and be ruled by mere chance? Secondly, if a good God exists why is there so much pain and suffering in human existence? Finally, if an all-knowing, all-powerful God exists, doesn't that compromise human freedom? If God knows in advance everything you're going to do, how could you act freely? Boethius's meditations on these issues proved enormously influential, both among professional philosophers but also among the literate public, his book being a medieval 'bestseller'.

A major influence on Boethius was Plato. Gwen Murphy discusses his contribution in her chapter. The figure of Plato looms large over the whole western intellectual tradition, whether through religious adaptations of his views or forthright rejection of his 'otherworldly' thought. Plato's thought is notoriously difficult to interpret and this chapter examines different ways of reading his work. One way is to systematise his work, setting up a theory which lends itself to the picture of the Platonic philosopher as an ethereal, academic, impractical dreamer with nothing of relevance to say to people struggling with real-life practical problems of existence. A different way emphasises the practical motivations of Plato's work, arguing that it is precisely directed towards such existential situations. The Platonic philosopher counters seductive, unreflective attractions which seem surprisingly contemporary – wealth, fame, pleasure – and argues that happiness is found in something more objective, less ephemeral. The key claim of this chapter is that Plato's message has ongoing relevance to problems of existence – it is not merely an idle academic speculative pastime.

Ciaran McGlynn presents the views of the Stoics, noting how they might seem to offer ideal remedies for current ills. Flourishing in classical Athenian and then Roman society, they devised a philosophy which was tooled exactly to deal with deep social change and to cope with the kind of turmoil which such change usually entails. Their thought was not primarily speculative, but dealt with questions of human happiness. They diagnosed the source of unhappiness in unruly emotions and counselled the path to true happiness in the control of those very emotions. It is not the way the world is that leads to unhappiness, it is how one reacts to that world that determines it. Everyone is familiar with the image of the unhappy miser who constantly seeks for more and the happy pauper who is carefree. So the ideal of someone who is freed from the vicissitudes of emotional travail is held up as the model for happiness. This has contemporary resonance in classic action heroes, such as James Bond, whose upper lip barely twitches as he shoots, cuts and bombs his way through plot after plot. Yet a recent twist to the familiar plotline makes Bond emotionally vulnerable and McGlynn questions whether the Stoic advice is really workable. Insensitivity to difficult emotion leads to a general emotional stultification which seems to cut off access to something which is important and distinctively human.

Concluding the engagement with the world of ancient philosophy, Brendan O'Byrne critiques contemporary consumerism, using tools from a number of ancient philosophers' reflections on desire. While an ancient ideal had been to curb desire, or achieve some kind of moderation as a means to happiness, consumerism turns this on its head. Drawing its inspiration from the late eighteenth century work of Jeremy Bentham, consumerism seeks to maximise consumption as the path to happiness. Unlike classical views advocating pleasure as a good which restricted its use to a small group, modern consumerism is distinctive in being a mass phenomenon. Now, apart from being ecologically unsustainable, it is argued here that this gets the picture of human happiness completely wrong. To counter it a kind of philosophy is required which is not simply an academic discipline. Rather the ancient notion of philosophy as a spiritual practice is appealed to.' Spiritual' here is not synonymous with 'religious', but refers rather to the thought that it is not merely something intellectual, a cerebral grasp of particular ideas, but a more comprehensive integration of thought, emotion, desire and community.

If O'Byrne has argued for a conception of philosophy which goes beyond the merely academic, Manfred Weltecke introduces the thought of the philosopher who stands for many as an archetype of the pure, academic, professorial kind of philosopher, Immanuel Kant. As Weltecke remarks 'Kant led a very uneventful life devoted exclusively to his philosophical work'. However, Kant's thought was revolutionary in its impact, challenging traditional conceptions of what philosophers do and radically reshaping the picture of the relationship of human thought to reality. Prior to Kant it was generally held that human thought was largely passive, absorbing information about an objective world about it.

After Kant, the mind seemed far more creative, actively structuring the world of our experience. This fed into the cultural movement known as Romanticism, which privileged the role of the imagination and of the creative genius. Kant's views on human happiness come in his reflections on philosophy of religion, which can only be understood by grasping his ethical work and his work on human knowledge. Weltecke presents these in systematic sequence, arriving at a view which he describes as ennobling and hopeful.

Peter Simons examines the consolations of atheism in his paper. It is sometimes imagined that religious belief has a monopoly on consolation, but Simons challenges this view. He notes the burdens of religious belief around sex, sin and salvation, arguing that being free of such burdens is itself a form of consolation. He sharply distinguishes questions of value from questions about God – it is possible to have reasoned discussions about ethics without having to assume a divine lawgiver. While shedding the idea that there is a divine retributive justice for people such as Hitler or Stalin might be unpleasant, it might also spur one to seek for this-worldly justice. There are also positive aspects to atheism (not merely leaving aside the burdens of religion). The world is purely gratuitous and is awe-inspiring, as is humanity. 'An atheist is just as well placed as any believer to appreciate the beauty of art and nature, the warmth of love and affection, the wonder of discovery, and the grandeur of the universe.' So, as well as defending the plausibility and attractiveness of atheism, Simons poses important challenges to those whose worldview is religious.

A different but related challenge comes from Donal McGinley's chapter on Buddhism. By many normal anthropological criteria, Buddhism counts as a religion, exhibiting ritual, prayer, institutional structures, beliefs and ethical standards associated with religious belief. Nevertheless the idea of God plays little role in it and is indeed rejected by many Buddhist thinkers. In recent years Buddhism has grown in the west among those seeking spiritual consolation but disaffected by institutional religion. McGinley discusses its history, worldview, characteristic beliefs and moral teaching. Among the topics discussed are challenges to Buddhism from a monotheistic perspective and the potential values which may arise from adopting certain Buddhist attitudes. But is Buddhism a philosophy? Part of the interest in looking at Buddhism is that it stretches our concepts of religion, philosophy, secularism, spirituality. McGinley says, 'At the very least, an acquaintance with Buddhist thought will allow us to think in a way that perhaps we have never thought before, exposing our minds to an alternative view of reality and of the possibilities for human society.'

From antiquity, there has been an awareness of the abstruseness and potential irrelevancy of certain kinds of philosophical discussion. Ciaran McGlynn discusses a philosophical system which is keenly attuned to that worry, pragmatism. Originating in 19th century American thought, it is a style of philosophy which attends very much to the practical ramifications of abstract thought and which appeals to human experience. McGlynn presents the work of William James and Richard Rorty, noting their common mistrust of speculation far removed from lived experience, but also noting their differences in temperament and interest. James is interested in religious issues, Rorty not. James has a greater regard for the role of science, Rorty is more radical in challenging the intellectual dominance of modern science. In this chapter some of the great contemporary debates in philosophy are raised. What is meant by notions such as 'truth', 'objectivity', 'reality'? Is there any such thing as absolute truth? Is the denial of such a notion incoherent (namely, it is absolutely true that there is no absolute truth?).

Of course, philosophy is not the only kind of thing which might console one in difficult circumstances. Money, the appreciation of art, humble cups of tea can all serve in different ways to console. Joseph McLoughlin looks at what makes philosophy distinctive among the different forms of consolation available. He particularly focuses on art, given that many seek and find consolation in differing art forms. But he argues that even there, one can find a role for philosophical reflection and he engages with an important theory about the function of art, deriving from the work of the 20th century English philosopher, R. G. Collingwood. Collingwood believed that art was peculiarly suited to help one clarify one's emotions. McLoughlin challenges this view and defends the notion of craft as having an essential and not merely subsidiary role in understanding art.

One of the most important jobs performed by philosophers is to challenge the consensus view, to make one reflect on and defend one's assumptions. It's what made Socrates so unpopular in Athens, where he likened his role to that of a stinging insect. In the final contribution, Paal Antonsen does exactly that. The whole thrust of this book is that philosophy can provide consolation in difficult times. Antonsen trenchantly argues that it does not and should not do so. On his account philosophy (in common with other academic subjects) aims at the truth, but this has no connection with any idea of consolation. To add consolation into the mix of the pursuit of truth is to court narcisissism and wishful thinking. Philosophy has no special status in teaching one how to live and while consolation can be found, it is to be found in collective social action – 'the consolation to be gained for oneself must be provided through consoling others'.

Conclusion

Because the questions it deals with are so fundamental, the means to answer them varied and the criteria for assessing the answers are controverted, there is no easy consensus to be found in philosophy. Some find this frustrating, wanting to clear away the tedious discussion to get the 'right' answer. Others find this liberating, believing that the world of theory offers creative and multifarious ways of helping one to live and understand one's place in the world. The chapters in this book represent the interests and reflections of an academic community, the Department of Philosophy at Trinity College Dublin, which devotes itself to the study, teaching and writing of philosophy. The influences, sources and backgrounds of the writers vary widely. What unites them (apart from all teaching there) is a belief in the importance of philosophical reflection and the desire to communicate some of that to as wide an audience as possible. Each chapter began as an evening lecture in an extra-mural course in the Michaelmas term of 2009 on the theme of the Consolations of Philosophy. That as wide-ranging, thought-provoking and stimulating a selection of essays emerged is a tribute to the healthy state of philosophy at TCD. For many of us, that in itself is a consoling thought!

CHAPTER ONE

Finding Consolation in God:
Boethius and The Consolation of Philosophy

Paul O'Grady

How the Book Came to be Written

The most famous instance of philosophy consoling someone in adversity is surely found in Boethius's *The Consolation of Philosophy* (*Philosophiae Consolationis*), written in 524 when its author was in prison awaiting execution. It is a work of philosophical theism, in that it presents a picture of the world governed by a non-physical creator who cares for his creation. This will function as the chief consolation for Boethius in his difficulties, the belief that there is a deep, benign, purpose or order to the world. Unlike other religious texts, in the *Consolation* Boethius doesn't appeal to revelation, church authority or putative personal religious experience to support this vision, but instead uses the resources of philosophy and argues that it is truly rational to hold such a view. Then, as now, there are obvious difficulties which strike even the most ardent supporter of such a picture. How does the fact of suffering fit into this view? If God is benevolent and all powerful, why is it that wicked people thrive and good people suffer? Furthermore, isn't such a picture of the relationship of God and humanity incoherent? If God has attributes such as being allknowing, how can there be human free will? God's knowledge is supposed to extend to all actions, so if God knows in advance about everything one does, how can one act freely? Boethius tackles these issues directly, attempting to learn from his own adversity and reconciling his circumstances with his conception of the nature of God, the world and human existence.

The book which resulted from his meditations in prison became a veritable bestseller in the medieval world. It was translated from Latin into the vernacular languages. King Alfred is attributed with the translation into Old English, Chaucer produced a famous version in Middle English and Queen Elizabeth the First produced a translation. Its echoes can be found in Dante, who uses famous Boethian images such as the wheel of fortune and the love that turns the sun and stars. Thomas Aquinas adopts Boethius's views on eternity and employs unmodified a metaphor of God in eternity as being on a mountain peak surveying time in the valleys below. Boethius, along with Augustine and Pseudo-Dionysius, was one of the main conduits for core ideas of ancient philosophy to the middle ages. Indeed one of his chief intellectual aims was to translate the works of the great Athenian philosophers, Plato and Aristotle, into Latin. He didn't succeed in completing this, but what he did translate was central to the medieval educational curriculum. And the *Consolation* itself was a crucial repository of ancient philosophical lore for the literate of the medieval period. It can be classified as a Neoplatonic work, one which takes Plato as its basic influence and which seeks to harmonise his philosophy with Aristotle and other subsequent philosophers.

Boethius (or Anicius Manlius Severinus Boethius to give his full name) was born into a noble Roman family, the Anicii, about 480 ce. His father, a consul, died while Boethius was a child and he was adopted by the head of the senate, Symmachus, who introduced him to a life of culture and study. He later married Symmachus's daughter, Rusticiana, becoming a consul himself and having two sons who also became consuls. Rome had fallen into the hands of Gothic kings in the late fifth century. His birth father had been consul to the Gothic king Odoacer, and Theodoric was king from 493-526, into whose service Boethius entered. Boethius's chief bent was towards scholarship, studying the liberal arts and philosophy. He was fluent in Greek, a skill becoming increasingly rare in his world (hence his translation project). However, coming to the attention of Theodoric, he was summoned into public service, eventually rising to *magister officiorum*, the head of the civil service. This required travel from Rome and attendance at court at Ravenna and Verona. Simultaneous with this administrative work was his scholarly output of translations of ancient authors, commentaries, treatises on logic, music, arithmetic and theology. With these alone he would have been a significant figure in the history of ideas, but the *Consolation* is what secured his place as a major philosopher.

The fourth and fifth centuries had witnessed significant theological controversy, which formed the backdrop to Boethius's imprisonment. One relevant factor in this was the division of the Church into Eastern and Western wings, the former based in Constantinople with an Emperor, the latter at Rome with a King and Pope. Political tensions existed between these poles. Another factor was the great theological debates about the Trinity, how to understand the conundrum of God being both one and three. Church councils at Nicea (325ce) and Chalcedon (451ce) had hammered out a vocabulary using philosophical terms such as person, nature, substance and procession to articulate the orthodox position. Yet the views of Arius (c250-336ce), who maintained that the second person of the Trinity, the Son, was a creature and not of the same status as the Father, were widespread and influential. The Goths were Arian and Theodoric ruled a kingdom in which Arians, Orthodox Christians and Jews lived peacefully together. Boethius was an orthodox Christian (writing a treatise on the Trinity), but was implicated in a treasonous plot to get the Eastern emperor to invade and squash the heretical Arian Theodoric. It seems as if the real impetus behind the attack on Boethius was court jealousy and he denied any treacherous correpondence. However, Theodoric was sensitive to his position being undermined by the Emperor, having Boethius exiled to imprisonment in Pavia and bludgeoned to death in 524. The *Consolation* was written in prison awaiting the sentence to be fully carried out. Hence the existential situation of Boethius, the author, is of one who is not merely fulfilling a scholarly exercise but of one giving testament to his fundamental and deeply cherished ideas.

These ideas are primarily drawn from Plato. The Neoplatonists had systematised Plato's thought and sought to downplay any disagreements with Aristotle. The world is viewed as a place amenable to rational investigation. The invisible infrastructure of such a world include forms, understood as intelligible archetypes or patterns of qualities. So, for example, justice existed as an abstract intangible reality, the pattern for all individual just acts. Absolute, abstract justice existed as an ideal, as did goodness, truth, beauty and so on. Plotinus (205-270ce) was the chief systematiser of Plato's sinuous ideas and emphasised the place of the One, the apex of the invisible hierarchy. This was the source and origin of all, which was beyond all categories, all rationalisation. The One was simple, undivided, perfect. What lay below it was multiple, divided and imperfect. On reaching the realm of matter, a level very low down in the hierarchical structure of reality was being considered. Subsequent religious advocates of this view grafted the Neoplatonist One onto the monotheistic conception of God. The patterns or archetypes became divine ideas. The problems of relating Plato's world to matter became the problem of relating creator to creation. Christian, Jewish and subsequently Islamic thinkers engaged in this process. Boethius found it natural to think of his Christian God in Neoplatonic terms. His influence on later Christian medieval thinkers such as Aquinas, Bonaventure and Scotus was great – generating a philosophical vocabulary in Latin, deriving from Greek antiquity, which served to shape the basic conceptual scheme in which they thought.

Philosophy and God

Boethius begins his book by depicting himself writing in prison. The text intersperses his prose with poetic passages and the opening section is a poem beginning, 'I who once composed with eager zest am driven by grief to shelter in sad songs' – bewailing his fate. After his dolorous opening he stands back a little from his writing and only then notices a woman standing over him in his cell. Her appearance is extraordinary – tall, ageless, keen-eyed, with distinctive clothing. This clothing is fine, skilfully wraught, but obscured with a film of dust, as from neglect. She bears the Greek letters *Pi* and *Theta* (signifying practical and speculative thought), but the clothing is torn – marauders having carried off bits of it. She speaks with authority and banishes the muses of poetry from sight, angrily saying that they were making Boethius worse rather than better. He doesn't recognise her and wonders at her authority. She, in turn, recites a poem to Boethius about his state of mind, how fallen it is, but tells him it is now a time for healing, not lamenting. He then recognises her, 'the clouds of my grief dissolved and I drank in the light' – she was his nurse from his youth – Philosophy.

This personification of philosophy is unusual in philosophical writing. In one sense it is clearly a literary device, in the same way as talk of muses are. Yet there are also strands of thought which feed into the idea that philosophy exists as an independent reality. The etymology of 'philosophy' connects it to *Sophia*, (Wisdom), and Boethius would have been aware of the Jewish tradition of treating wisdom as feminine and as an agent of God. The so-called Wisdom literature, which includes Proverbs and the Book of Wisdom, speaks of Wisdom as existing before the creation of the world, as the oldest of God's works (see Proverbs 8). But later there is the question of whether Wisdom is actually to be identified with God, as in the famous opening of John's gospel, 'In the beginning was the Word and and Word was God'. The Greek term used there, *Logos*, has multiple meanings, including 'word', 'meaning', 'explanation', 'wisdom' and is one which dominated the thought of early Greek philosophers. Biblical scholars are in agreement that the Johannine author took the idea from the Jewish tradition, not the Greek. So Wisdom and God coalesce in that work. In Boethius's work, philosophy operates as a path to God, offering therapy in his time of distress.

Recently, a number of psychotherapists have looked back to classical philosophers for inspiration in their art. Irvin Yalom, a practitioner of Existential Psychotherapy, has written a book extolling the Epicureans and using their ideas to confront death anxiety.[1] As the fear of death is deep in us, but hard to look at, Yalom entitled his book *Staring at the Sun* and discusses ways of minimising fear of death (including some of those discussed by Peter Simons in his essay). The Epicureans (and Yalom) were atheists and so their therapy drew on themes such as freedom, creativity and lack of an afterlife. Philosophy, in Boethius, agrees that a correct view of reality helps healing, but her substantive views are different from Yalom's. For Boethius, understanding

1. Irvin Yalom, *Staring at the Sun*, Jossey-Bass, San Francisco, 2008

the true nature of himself, the true nature of fortune, abandoning false cures and undergoing the rigours of correct reasoning lie at the heart of Philosophy's regimen. Her mere appearance was enough to draw Boethius away from blind grief and back to the path of reason and she speaks of bringing him along a path of more and more stringent treatment.

As Philosophy brings Boethius to regain his equilibrium, the discussion of the existence of God is fairly perfunctory. There are no elaborate arguments of the kind found in Augustine, Anselm, Aquinas or Scotus. Rather she puts a direct question to him: 'Do you believe that this life consists of haphazard and chance events, or do you think it is governed by some rational principle?' He replies: 'I could never believe that events of such regularity are due to the haphazards of chance. In fact I know that God the Creator watches over His creation. The day will never come that sees me abandon the truth of this belief' [1.6]. And that's it. Pretty much everthing else in his book flows from that affirmation. Much subsequent philosophical wrangling has taken place over whether the existence of regularity or order is evidence for the existence of God, and even whether conceding a rational principle is the same as conceding God (maybe some impersonal force, as in Taoism, rather than the Judaeo-Christian God is in question). Many think that Darwinism has put paid to such reasoning, insofar as Darwin shows how order can arise precisely through the haphazards of chance. And given that Darwin has a very high degree of rational credibility, it seems that reasoning of the kind advanced by Boethius has been swept aside by scientific advance. Notwithstanding claims of that kind, the kind of order appealed to by Boethius is of a different kind to that which Darwinians attack. They can explain the complexity of organisms in the physical world. But they don't explain the deep structures of the physical universe – e.g. gravitation, strong and weak nuclear attraction, the amenability of the world to quantitative analysis. Indeed the existence of sexual reproduction is not explained, insofar as evolutionary explanation presupposes it. So the easy Darwinian dismissal of Boethius's intuition is not convincing. The great Scottish philosopher David Hume (1711-1776) posed more profound challenges to such arguments, but this is not the place to discuss them.[2] Suffice for the moment to note that Boethius accepts readily that the world is ordered and rational and that God sustains and orders it. A different but pressing problem for him is the following:

> It is nothing short of monstrous that God should look on while every criminal is allowed to achieve his purpose against the innocent. If this is so, it was hardly without reason that one of your household asked where evil comes from if there is a god and where good comes from if there isn't. [I.4]

In this Boethius refers to the classic challenge of Epicurus about the compatibility of God and evil. In his incarceration, it is an even more pressing problem for him and I shall address it in the next section.

A deep puzzle surrounds Boethius's discussion of God. Given that he is a practising Christian and that part of the reason for his imprisonment is theological, there is a complete absence of any specifically Christian element in the work. One might expect some reflections on the passion, death and resurrection of Christ, but it is completely absent. Why is this? There is no satisfactory answer available. Some suggest that since the book is called *The Consolation of Philosophy*, it would be inappropriate for Boethius to discuss such topics. But this just pushes the puzzle back to why then write such a book, rather than an explicitly Christian text? Some question Boethius's real beliefs and argue that he is, in fact, a pagan philosopher. But this doesn't square with his other writings and the facts of his biography. Furthermore, the God he believes in is construed personally, not an impersonal cosmic force, so his theism is genuine. Probably the most famous poem, or hymn, in the work opens:

> O Thou who dost by everlasting reason rule,
> Creator of the planets and the sky, who time
> From timelessness did bring, unchanging Mover,
> No cause drove thee to mould unstable matter, but
> The form benign of highest good within Thee set.

2. Hume

All things Thou bringest forth from Thy high archetype:
Thou height of beauty, in Thy mind the beauteous world
Dost bear, and in that ideal likeness shaping it,
Dost order perfect parts a perfect whole to frame.[III.9]

In this worldview, Boethius joins with Plato, Aristotle, Philo, Plotinus, Proclus, Avicenna, Averroes and Maimonides, a tradition of pagan Greek, Jewish and Islamic thinkers, who believed that philosophy can shed some light on God. It is a tradition which fed into Christian theology with Augustine, Anselm and Aquinas. It has fallen out of favour both in philosophy in general and more specifically in Christian theology. Part of the reason for its philosophical fall from favour was skepticism about metaphysics of this kind, deriving from Hume and Kant, a skepticism which dominated modern thought, but which has weakened in recent decades. Part of the reason for its theological dismissal has been the widespread capitulation of that discipline to forms of postmodern skepticism, which denies the possibility of having some rationally based coherent overarching view of reality. One can frequently find attempts to give a reason-based acount of God dismissed by theologians as exempifying Enlightenment views of reason, views held to be mistaken. Yet Boethius stands as an example of a tradition much older than the Enlightenment which saw its chief task as doing precisely that, applying reason to questions about God.

The Problem of Evil

Boethius describes his suffering in prison. Not only is there the incarceration, the lack of freedom, the impending threat of death, but also the sting that it is wholly undeserved, that he is the victim of the wickedness of others. This is the condition in which Philosophy encounters him and to which she applies her remedies. She gets him to think of the good things which still remain to him – his privileged origins, his successful life, his wife, his children. Many would consider him extremely fortunate for all these goods. She points out that no-one escapes the vicissitudes of fate, in every life there are upturns and downturns, it is the nature of the human condition. Indeed, Boethius is experiencing the first real trial of his life, so far everything has gone his way. In an anticipation of a theme which will surface again in Milton and in Sartre, Philosophy says: 'Nothing is miserable except when you think it so, and vice versa, all luck is good luck to the man who bears it with equanimity' [II.4] Pressing home her point, she argues that happiness cannot be found outside oneself, it always lies within. It doesn't consist in things governed by chance, it is more stable than that. Happiness is not a matter of temperament or disposition, but a matter of having correct beliefs. She contends that most people have incorrect views about the nature of happiness, giving a list of the typical things people think will make them happy – wealth, high office, power, fame, physical pleasures.

Philosophy forensically tackles each one of these and displays its shortcomings. Wealth doesn't make one self-sufficient, indeed the opposite. One cannot ensure it will not be taken away, one seeks outside help to protect it. The kind of wants which money assuages don't go away, they just need constant feeding. Riches create wants of their own (recall the old joke – 'What do you give the person who has everything? More!'). High office might then offer a better hope of happiness, getting honour and respect for the holder. However, rather than removing wickedness, high office often seems to bring it under scrutiny, bringing it to light, many in high office can be seen to be venal. It is not the high office itself which confers respect, but the kind of person who holds it. It is also the case that the recognition of high office varies widely, (foreigners may stare blankly at local dignitaries) showing that it is not an inherent property like the heating power of fire, but a much more ephemeral thing. Political power is insufficient for its own preservation – history is full of anxious despots seeking vainly to hold on, all ending like Ozymandias the Great in Shelley's famous poem. Likewise, cronies of the powerful are in an even more precarious position – Seneca was forced to kill himself by Nero whose friend he had been. Fame – the drug of choice of the early twenty-first century – is summarily dismissed by Philosophy since it is often based on false opinion, is fortuitous and fleeting. Finally physical pleasure comes last on the list, 'its pursuit is full of anxiety and its fulfilment full of remorse' [III.7]. All these roads to happiness are dismissed as sidetracks.

What, then, is the nature of true happiness? One can deduce it from the failure of false paths, being the opposite of them. It is what confers self-sufficiency, strength, makes one worthy of true respect and is glorious and joyful. Nothing mortal and mutable can do this task. Happiness is to be found in goodness, while God and true goodness are identified. Philosophy presents a strongly Platonic vision of a world where goodness is a real, absolute reality which exists timelessly and non physically. God is the seat of this true goodness – God is good by nature. All other things are good by participation in this true goodness. Happiness is sharing in this goodness. The goal of human existence is sharing in God's goodness and this is true happiness. Yet in the face of this calm disquisition on Platonic philosophy, Boethius regroups one more time in the name of common-sense and presents once again the problem of evil. He complains that not only do the wicked flourish but they tread down good people and this flies in the face of a supposedly good God.

A number of surprising corrollories arise from the position Philosophy has outlined, which answer Boethius's impassioned outbursts about the success of evildoers. Philosophy reasons with him that while all people seek the good, only some achieve it. The wicked follow a mistaken picture of the good, while the virtuous actually succeed in reaching it. The wicked either are ignorant of the true good, or else know it but are unable to achieve it, through weakness of will or excessive appetite. The goodness of good people cannot be taken away, while wickedness is actually a deficiency, deserving of pity. Boethius, not surprisingly, says that 'when I turn to the opinions of ordinary men, few would even grant you a hearing, let alone believe you' [IV.4]. Philosophy agrees, but says this is because they only look to their desires, not to the order of creation. She maintains a strong line on the reality of absolute goodness and the counterintuitive fact that those who commit an injustice are more unhappy than those who suffer it.

Boethius still voices his misgivings when he says:

> I would be less surprised if I could believe that the confusion of things is due to the fortuitous operations of chance. But my wonder is only increased by the knowledge that the ruling

power of the universe is God. Sometimes He is pleasant to the good and unpleasant to the bad, and other times He grants the bad their wishes and denies the good. But since He often varies between these two alternatives, what grounds are there for distinguishing between God and the haphazards of chance? [IV.5]

This leads to a discussion of God's providence for the world and how it relates to chance. Philosophy (smilingly) describes this as the greatest of all questions, involving the oneness of providence, the course of fate, the haphazard nature of random events of chance, divine knowledge and predestination and the freedom of the will and says it will take really lively intellectual fire to deal with them. The final part of the *Consolation* deals with such issues (from IV. 6 to V.6).

Providence, Fate and Eternity

Philosophy holds that God orders all things, but this can be viewed in two ways. One way is thinking of it as existing in God, unified in the divine mind, and this is called Providence. The other way is to think of this plan existing in time, operating through multifarious causes in the world and in history, and this is called Fate. Humans are in no position to grasp the overall providential plan, but instead see Fate as it unfolds itself in time. Philosophy contends that what Fate metes out to each individual is part of God's providence, but it is unclear to humans how the plan works out well. Providence gives reward and punishment, training and discipline. Hardship offers the possibility of self discovery and the virtuous should view distress as an opportunity.

Boethius asks whether chance has any role to play in this view of reality? Philosophy responds that chance can mean different things. If by chance is meant simply the coming into existence of something out of nothing, she denies this and affirms the thought that nothing comes out of nothing. However, if by chance is meant the fact that some actions which are performed for a particular purpose actually result in unintended consequences, then this exists. It is due to the causes of an event being conjoined with action to some purpose which results in something unforseen,

such as digging one's garden to plant vegetables but finding trea-
sure.

Boethius then wonders whether it is possible for there to be
free will in this situation. If providence rules the world and causal
laws operate rigidly throughought creation, how can one act
freely? Philosophy initially replies by affirming the reality of free
will, maintaining that it is fundamental for any rational being that
free will exists and morality couldn't exist without it. But Boethius
responds that there seems to be an incompatibility between God's
universal knowledge and free will. If God knows in advance what
is going to happen and God's knowledge is infallible, then whatever he knows has to happen. God knew that you, reader, would
read this very sentence at this very moment, and so there was no
possibility that you didn't, that you might have skipped this section, or wandered off to make a cup of tea. Because God knew it
from eternity, it *had* to happen. So how can there be free will?

Philosophy acknowledges the antiquity of this problem, noting that Cicero had tackled it. She gets to the nub of the problem by
saying that if there wasn't any foreknowledge, the actions of the
will wouldn't be predestined, to which Boethius agrees. And she
adds that even if there was foreknowledge but it didn't predestine
action, there still would be freedom of the will. Puzzledly he accepts this.

Philosophy now makes two moves. Firstly she defends the
view that things known are known in a way determined by the
kind of thing which knows them. In other words, the knower is
vital in knowledge, rather than the object known. Secondly she argues that God's manner of knowing is significantly different to
the human manner of knowing. Putting these two together, she
claims that God's knowledge of all things doesn't entail predeter-
minism and blocks human free will. So let's examine how she does
this.

She argues that the senses grasp objects in different ways, e.g.
seeing a ball is different to touching it. Seeing a human is different
to imagining one, or thinking about one. Part of this difference is
qualitative – reasoning is more universal and superior to imagining or sensing (for example, your cat can be trained to recognise a

triangle using sense knowledge, but can't do trigonometry). She then contends that there is an intellect higher than the human which knows in a fashion superior to human thought, but humans typically suppose that theirs is the model of all knowledge.

What is distinctive of this intellect is that it is eternal – it doesn't exist in time. Eternity is defined as 'the complete, simultaneous and perfect possession of everlasting life' [V.6]. It is an interesting definition, as nothing much to do with time is involved in it. A typical thought about eternity is that it is everlasting time, without beginning or end. But this definition differs. Whatever is eternal is alive. It also is in full contact with all of itself – it has not lost the past nor anticipates the future. This contrasts with something which might exist forever in time (as the ancient philosophers believed about the physical world), it still has a past and a future. Eternity is a kind of existence which contrasts with temporal existence. God's existence is eternal, creation exists in time.

God's knowledge of the world is eternal. Past, present and future are all present to God in a single eternal instant. He knows things as they happen. Some of those things are necessary, they have to be (for example water being H2O), but some are not, your reading this. Philosophy uses the analogy of vision. Everything presently happening is necessary in the sense that it can't be otherwise as it happens, it swiftly becomes the past, which is fixed. However, among the things which happen, some are necessary (like the chemical constitution of water), some aren't (you reading). Anyone looking at you reading knows that you are reading and that it can't be otherwise – but that doesn't mean that you had no freedom not to read. You could have decided to jog and anyone watching you freely jog is observing a free action. Philosophy argues that God's knowledge is similar to this. He knows actions as they happen, but this doesn't prevent them from being freely chosen. Strictly speaking, God does not have foreknowledge, his eternal knowledge is outside time and cannot, as a matter of logic, be before or after anything. This allows freedom of the will. Philosophy finishes with a stern warning to Boethius to be good, since he is under the constant gaze of the eternal God.

Conclusion

There are several paradoxes to Boethius's book. At the start, Philosophy banishes the muses of poetry, yet there are 42 lengthy poems dotted through the text. As mentioned above he is a devout Christian, yet nothing specifically Christian enters the text. As an author defending a theistic view of reality, he makes himself, the literary character Boethius, express the deepest problems with such a vision. Whether he is ultimately convinced is not stated – the character Boethius gets to say one word ('No') in the climactic final chapter – V.6, otherwise Philosophy is in full flight.

Is the *Consolation* relevant or convincing in a modern age? The three great positive objections[3] to theistic belief are 1) the redundancy of God in a scientific age, 2) the problem of evil, 3) the incoherence of theism. Boethius attempts to get one to think in a metaphysical fashion about the basic structure of reality. He presents a vision of a world made and governed by God, one compatible with scientific advances and discoveries, with God as the basic condition of intelligibility of such a world. He tackles the problem of evil head on, arguing that we may not have a correct grasp of what actually constitutes genuine goodness and that suffering may not be pointless. Finally he argues that the traditional view of God as all knowing does not prevent one from holding to free will.

His relative lack of interest in arguing for God's existence no doubt reflects his intellectual environment, where it was pretty much accepted by everyone, unlike today's intellectual climate. The real power in his writing comes from attempting to resolve puzzles for anyone who accepts such a worldview. It is by no means obvious that his discussion of apparent versus genuine goodness or of the relation of time to something beyond time have been made redundant by scientific advances. His book can still serve as a starting point for those who believe in some form of benign non-physical reality underpinning and sustaining the world

---

3. One might think that negative objections are those which attack arguments advanced by theists to show that God exists, for example Hume's attacks on the argument to design. Positive objections are separate atheistic claims designed to show the lack of coherence or explanatory inadequacy of the idea of God, for example the problem of evil.

and who struggle to make sense of that picture given the vicissitudes of human existence.

Further Reading
Boethius, *The Consolation of Philosophy*, Penguin Classics, 2003
Kenny, A., *Medieval Philosophy: A New History of Western Philosophy*, Vol 2, Oxford 2007
Marenbon, J., *Boethius*, Oxford, 2003

CHAPTER TWO

Consolation from Plato

Gwen Murphy

*Imagine a dark, subterranean prison in which humans are bound by
their necks to a single place from infancy. Elaborate steps are taken by
unseen forces to supply and manipulate the content of the prisoners'
experience. This is so effective that the prisoners do not recognise
their imprisonment and are satisfied to live their lives in this way.
Moreover, the cumulative effects of this imprisonment are so thorough that if freed, the prisoners would be virtually helpless. It is not
unreasonable to expect that some prisoners would wish to remain im-
prisoned even after their minds grasped the horror of their condition.
But if a prisoner was dragged out and compelled to understand the
true nature of his imprisonment, matters would be different. In time
the prisoner would come to have a knowledge far superior to that
based on the images that made up the whole of experience before. This
freed prisoner would understand those images as illusory. His life
would never be the same again.*[1]

Plato's allegory of the cave is perhaps one of the best-known
images in philosophy, but what he wishes to convey through
these images is a highly contestable issue. To some, Plato is telling
us to step back, epistemologically, from this sense-perceptible
world around us so we can get a better view of the real world – the
World of Forms. For most commentators in the English-speaking
world, Plato advocates a life of theoretical contemplation, dedicated to finding the ultimate meaning of reality through coming
to know the forms. However, work done in the natural sciences
has called into question the very possibility of such a project.
According to naturalism, the philosophical view that the 'only
reality is nature',[2] we have no right to demand 'The Truth' from a

1. Adapted from *The Republic* (514a-517d)
2. www.naturalisms.org

world so evidently governed by contingency and chance. We should graciously accept our situation as an accident of evolution and give up these vain attempts to find some grand narrative that explains the meaning of it all.

When the possibility of truth is denied, a life dedicated to the pursuit of pleasure comes to the fore as a viable alternative. If all we are is a body, the soul having been dispersed alongside all other non-natural entities, then satisfying the wants of the body seems a good way to live. But before we dedicate too much time to this appetitive lifestyle, Plato asks that we first pause and reflect on the nature of this life; not by turning away from this world, but through inquiring into the nature of our lives as we live them here and now and into the form or character the things that mean the most to us have – justice, courage, beauty and so on. These forms only become meaningful through the search, and as the philosopher searches his life grows in meaning. The Platonic philosopher turns away from wandering around in a world of opinion and hearsay so he can fill his life with meaning; and, as his life becomes richer and deeper in meaning, so too does his love of wisdom.[3] This is the message behind the allegory of the cave.

This paper examines both readings of Plato, the metaphysical and the existential, and argues that the latter reading is preferable not only because it is more in keeping with the dialogues but because this form of Platonism reveals our ability to live a meaningful existence – without any need to search for The Truth 'out there' (wherever that is). This paper begins, however, with an exploration into the full implications of our modern, naturalist assumptions.

Why not satisfy the appetites?
Advocates of philosophical naturalism proclaim that our modern naturalistic understanding of the world has revealed to us something that has consumed philosophers for millennia – the true nature of our existence. It turns out that we are in fact nothing other than clever monkeys; creatures with no more of a guarantee of achieving happiness and fulfilment than any other of our simian cousins. True fulfilment and grand narratives explaining the ulti-

---

3. Philosophy (*philosophia*) literally means 'the love of wisdom'

mate nature of the universe and of life have been shown to be the misplaced dreams of philosophers and mystics, and have been rendered obsolete. We are simply one more thing in a world of things, subject to the same whims of nature and evolution as everything else. Mother Nature cares as much about our existence, our happiness and fulfilment, as she does about anything else in this universe – not a single jot.

Even so, it would appear she has a strange sense of humour with regard to this highly evolved mammalian species. Evolution has granted us powerful cognitive capacities that allow us to predict, control and manipulate our environment to an extent unrivalled by anything else in the animal kingdom. Unfortunately (or so it seems to the naturalists) the cerebral nature of our existence has left us with an unfortunate side-effect, sometimes referred to as 'existential angst', which has lead to our human preoccupation with trying to find some meaning, some grand truth, to explain why we are here in the first place (the family dog, in contrast, does not tend to stay in his basket all day because he cannot bear the thought of another twenty-four hours in a menial, servile existence). Since its dawning, the fight against this angst has taken many forms – from building pyramids to building philosophical systems. Our search for meaning, for a truth 'out there' which explains our existence, is an unavoidable consequence of the realisation that we exist. History would suggest that we cannot evade this feeling that it all must mean something; that there must be some point to it all.

However, our modern intellect, enriched by the facts that come from the natural sciences, has had to come to terms with the futility of this mission. For if we are no more than a (quite small) cog in the natural order of things, then we have no more right to demand some ultimate meaning in our lives than any other creature in the natural world. We are simply a contingent accident of evolution, a creature whose life is subject to forces beyond our control. Throw into the mix the societal forces that move our lives in ways we would not choose and we begin to understand Hobbes' synopsis of our existence as 'nasty, brutish and short'.[4]

---

4. Chapter XIII 'Of the Natural Condition of Mankind as Concerning Their Felicity and Misery' in *The Leviathan*

The wish to find some ultimate meaning in all of this is hardly surprising but the inevitability of this desire does not make the search for a truth 'out there' any less futile. This is the sad but unavoidable conclusion of our modern naturalistic worldview (the cave is all we have).

To find any happiness or satisfaction in this life we must turn away from philosophy and look elsewhere. In a life devoid of ultimate meaning, the satisfaction of bodily pleasures comes to the fore as a viable alternative. The search for meaning cannot help but be unsuccessful so instead of wasting our efforts on a fruitless quest for 'Truth' we should concentrate on being happy and contented on a smaller scale; seeking pleasure in the simple things in life – a beer, a movie or perhaps a warm body. Fortunately for us, this new naturalistic awareness has arisen in a society filled with pleasant and entertaining distractions; our modern Western perspective may have awoken us to the meaningless of our existence but at least it has given us the means to overcome any despair this thought may induce in any who feel compelled to search for something that is just not there. And, if we fail to find pleasure in one distraction, there is always a multitude of others to choose from; consumerist society runs on its ability to offer us a wide variety of distractions to entertain and amuse us.

This identification of a 'good life' with a life of pleasure is hardly a new idea.[5] And, so the argument goes, if a few pleasures can give us a little happiness then a life *filled* with pleasure will also be filled with happiness. A life of luxury has for millennia been lauded as the truly happy existence[6] – but our yearning for this life has an advantage over the Ancients, as only now is it fully realisable to even the commonest of men (if one only works hard enough or is lucky enough to win the lottery). And even if we fail to wallow in luxurious ease at least we can satisfy the appetites on whatever scale our wallet allows – and during the last few affluent years we managed to satisfy quite a few. But then the consequences of a

---

5. See, for example, the *Gorgias*
6. The Greek poet Simonides (c. 556 BC-468 BC) is reported to have said that it is better to be rich than to be wise, because wise men are found at the courts of the rich.

global overspend caught up with us and we now have less resources to spend on living an appetitive lifestyle. Before we climb
back on board the so-called 'boom and bust' rotation of modern
economics, hoping to once more procure the funds to live a pleasurable life, maybe we should pause for a moment and consider
whether this is indeed a 'good life'.

Caring for our souls
Plato places great weight and emphasis on the importance of examining and amending our beliefs about the world and our place
in it. Platonism rests on the very basic assumption that we need to
know what is good in order to know if we are making our life any
better through our actions. Mere appearances are not enough
when it comes to making our lives better – we may be content to
appear beautiful or courageous without being so in fact, but when
it comes to our lives, we want what is *really* good and not just what
looks good to others from the outside. A life of pleasure is sought
because it is thought to enhance the quality of our lives, not make
them worse. Plato's presumably uncontroversial claim is that
human beings always, and only, desire what is good for us. And,
as everyone desires this good, so, obviously, everyone needs to
know what this good is. The money and time invested in the
Western world on self-improvement and self-help manuals– all
offering the means to a better economic and / or spiritual life – appear to make this an equally uncontroversial claim.

But Plato thinks we are a little muddled in our methods, leading to notions of what is good which are at best confused and inadequate and at their worse misleading and dangerous. We start by
presuming to know what is good for us – wealth, power, sex or
sloth, for example – and then direct all our attention and energy
towards achieving that good. But a little reflection shows that
these things are only instrumental goods; for example, possessing
all the money in a post-apocalyptic, anarchic world without cur-
rency would do us very little good. The instrumental status of
these 'goods' grant even the most incontrovertible e.g. health and
wealth, with the power to cause damage and disruption to our
lives, for in possessing these 'goods' we have more opportunities

to do wrong than if we were cursed with a life of illness and poverty.[7] We confusingly desire the instruments themselves, making their possession a sufficient condition for happiness, when what we actually desire is the good we think they will bring. Yet, there is an insistence in modern thought that we know what will do us good without any reflection whatsoever.[8] The *Apology*, a dialogue in which Plato's mentor Socrates is sentenced to death, can be read as a single impassioned plea to make these reflections the primary concern in all our lives.

> You see, what I am doing as I go about is just trying to persuade both the young and the old among you not to care about bodies and money before, or as intensely as, you care about getting your souls in the best possible condition.
> *Apology 30a*

To the modern Western mind, influenced as it is by Christian beliefs, the soul is intrinsically linked to notions of human morality, but the soul (*psuché*) in Ancient Greece had a much broader range of incarnations. The soul was not primarily an ethical or moral concept in Greek thought, nor was mankind considered the only creatures to have a soul. Rather, *psuché* is the 'principle of life in men and animals', with Aristotle even suggesting that vegetables have souls.[9] The human soul includes all the non-physical elements that make up who we are – our will, desires and passions, our mind, reason and understanding. The virtues (*aretai*)[10] that make a soul good are as diverse in number as the variety of souls – the virtues of a good horse, for example, are very different from the virtues of an excellent onion.[11]

---

7. This is not to say that health and wealth are bad either; I am not advocating a life of poverty and sickness. The thought is, rather, that these things are neither good nor bad by themselves – they only become so when they are used beneficially or to our determent; and to do the former while avoiding the latter requires knowledge of the good.

8. See Brecher, 1998

9. R. E. Allen, 1996, p 92

10. The Greek word *areté* can be translated as either excellence or virtue – thus, the presence of certain virtues (*aretai* [*areté* plural]) in a thing together make up the excellence (*areté*) of that thing.

11. This is not to say that two different objects cannot share the same virtue; for example, both excellent horses and greyhounds share the virtue of speed.

Unsurprisingly, the search into what is good for us requires an investigation into the nature of those virtues relevant to the human life. So, in finding out what is good for us, we need to know the form or character of these virtues and this is what Plato is searching for. When Plato is searching for the forms (*eidoi*) of justice, courage etc, he is seeking out the nature or character these things have. As generally used, the Greek words *eidos* and *idea*, which are translated as 'form' and 'idea', mean the 'form, nature or character of a thing'. The *eidos* of a thing is the nature or quality that thing has in order to be that very thing e.g. the *eidos* of a triangle must include the fact that it is a three-sided shape. A horse-breeder should have a good knowledge of the virtues of an excellent horse, while those searching into the nature of the good life should have some knowledge of the things that make a human life good.

We start to take care of our souls when we are no longer comfortable with basing our happiness on the truths and opinions of others – casting off, as it were, the prisoner chains that bind us. Turning away from the empty shells of another's truth, we commence the inquiry for ourselves into what will do us good. Naturally, this investigation encompasses those virtues that make human life good. And guiding this search, lighting up the way as it were, is the form of the good – the form that gives truth and being to all the other forms, 'for how can one claim that a particular [object, action or event] is just, beautiful, courageous etc, unless it is also, in actuality, good?'[12] The form of the good is the highest of all forms as it is at the pinnacle of the search – we are searching into the nature of a good life, and is the form that makes the search possible. Leaving the cave, the philosopher begins his journey from darkness to light.

> The release from the bonds, the turning around from the shadows to the statues and the light of the fire and, then, the way up out of the cave to the sunlight … [philosophy] has the power to awaken the best part of the soul and lead it upward to the study of the best among the things that are. *Republic 532b6-8, c3-6*

---

12. Rowe, 2007, p 78

The problematic popular understanding of Plato
The allegory of the cave offers the reader a beautiful vision of the Platonic journey from ignorance to knowledge, culminating in knowledge of that most grandiose of Forms – The Good. However, the relation of such an exalted and lofty philosophy to life as it is lived may not be immediately obvious to those with some familiarity with Platonism. Trying to combine the stately vision of Platonic philosophy, as it is popularly understood, with the practical affair of everyday living may seem problematic at best – downright foolish at worst. Furthermore, this search has all the hallmarks of the futile quests mentioned earlier in this paper. The story, according to this tradition, goes something like this:

The Socratic plea to look after our souls, through the pursuit of the good, in the *Apology* is all well and good. Both Socrates and Plato want to convince us of the importance of caring for our souls and that the best, the only, way to achieve this goal is for us to live philosophically. But Socrates, by his own confession, was not particularly successful at the whole 'gaining knowledge' thing and, at the time of his death, found himself to be, more or less, in exactly the same state he was in at the beginning of his philosophical journey – as a know-nothing. He adamantly denied possessing any wisdom except, of course, the knowledge of his own ignorance.[13] Admittedly, the wisdom we are after is a special kind of knowledge, but this is knowledge of The Good and not our own ignorance. Acknowledging our own ignorance may be a necessary first step but, surely, there has to be more to philosophy than that. Small wonder, then, that the pupil, Plato, had to move past the master in his search for philosophical truth.

This move happens in the middle dialogues, which include the *Republic*, the dialogue which introduces the allegory of The Cave. Scholars have extracted from the pages of these dialogues 'the essence' of Platonism – the Theory of Forms. Plato, according to this theory, distrusted the sense-perceptible world around us (the cave); being in a state of constant flux, the objects in this world can never provide us with the knowledge that we seek. The true ob-

---

13. Socrates famously claimed to be more knowledgeable than anyone else only because he, unlike other people, knew that he was ignorant.

jects of knowledge must be stable and always the same if we are to stand any chance of knowing them, therefore these objects must be different from the sense-perceptible objects around us. Aristotle, in recounting Plato's intellectual development, informs us that 'Socrates was the first to seek the universal in ethical matters but he did not separate it. Plato, marrying Socrates' philosophy with that of Heraclitus, separated the universal, on the grounds that the sensible order, where Socrates had focused, was in flux' and Plato called these separated universals 'Forms' (*Metaphysics, 1078b12-34*).

In Aristotle's wake, scholars focus their attention on Plato's separation of universals and attempt to reconstruct how Plato conceived of this separation. This dedicated scholarship has manifested results in the form of the 'two-world' interpretation of Platonism. Plato, according to this story, postulated the existence of a world of Forms, containing those true objects of knowledge, standing over and above the sense-perceptible world around us. This physical world and all of its occupants are a copy or image of the Forms and since all copies are dependant on the original, this physical world is dependent on the realm of Forms. Accordingly, things in this realm attain reality only when 'partaking' of the Forms (a notoriously problematic relation for Platonic scholars).

The continuously shifting nature of the physical realm precludes the possibility of gaining knowledge through associating with it and demotes our epistemic relationship to one of mere belief. The goal of philosophy, to gain *knowledge*, can only be realised when the philosopher turns his back on this tumultuous mass and raises his gaze towards the Forms; those timeless, changeless beings that constitute what is *really* real. Philosophy is the study of these essences, beings whose existence depends on nothing but themselves, and The Good. And the highest, most exultant of these forms is, of course, the Form of the Good. The philosopher is one who has left the cave behind and has emerged to bask in the exquisite light of the Good. Plato, on this reading, is an otherworldly metaphysician, advocating a life dedicated to the contemplation of pure being as the best life possible.

The new metaphysics, according to these interpreters, provides Plato with a stable set of objects, an entire 'intelligent world over and above the sensible', to be accessed, mapped and explored by the philosopher, escaping from the fluxing world of particulars. (Rowe, 2007, 41)

As beautiful, magnificent, and metaphysically and epistemologically meaty as this may be, it is hardly practical. Those with the appropriate desire, time and resources to devote their life to boundless cogitation may well find they are living 'the good life' but we cannot all dedicate our lives to the study of the academic discipline of philosophy (a life that hardly seems practical, even on its own merits). How any of this is supposed to make our lives, as we live them in the *real world*, any better is far from obvious. It is hard to see how any of this relates in any way to making my life, as I live it here and now, any better. Furthermore, this Platonic search for Truth somewhere 'out there' would seem to be a particularly heinous example of the fanciful flights of philosophers much maligned in the first section of this paper.

This traditional reading, which flows from the commentary of Aristotle, however, fails to account for Plato's continued interest, from first dialogue to last, in a philosophy that is more than merely speculative. The value of philosophy lies, for Plato, in its foundational role in cultivating the best *society* and best *life* – neither of which can be achieved through escaping, by means of philosophy or anything else, from life and society as it is lived in this world. Truth and wisdom have value because they lead the philosopher towards the good *life*. The practical desiderata of life prevent the pursuit of truth from ever being 'purely academic'. Platonism, *as conceived by Plato*, champions a philosophy that can enrich the lives not only of scholars but the lives of *everyone*.[14] The character of Socrates is quite clear about this in the *Apology* when he says 'what I am doing as I go about is just trying to persuade both the young and the old among you [i.e. among the ordinary citizens of Athens] not to care about bodies and money before, or

14. Interestingly, there were not only male but also female philosophers in Plato's Academy. To say that this respect for the cognitive capacities of women was unusual in Ancient Greece would be to understate the case somewhat.

as intensely as, you care about getting your souls in the best possible condition' *(30a)*. Understanding Plato as advocating a scholastic life, dedicated to the contemplation of a World of Forms, which exists beyond this faulty world of the senses, misunderstands three, not inconsequential, aspects of Platonic philosophy: i) the nature of the forms, ii) the nature of philosophy and iii) the nature of the philosopher. A less than traditional explication of Plato will now be offered in answer to these problems.

Platonism and Life
To begin, it should be noted that Plato never actually offers us anything that even vaguely resembles a *theory* or *doctrine* of Forms. In his *Plato's Middle Period Metaphysics and Epistemology*, Allen Silverman laments:

> Unfortunately, neither in the *Phaedo* nor in any other dialogue do we find Plato giving a detailed description of the nature of the Forms, or particulars, or their interaction. What is referred to as Plato's theory of Forms is thus *a rational reconstruction* [my emphasis] of Plato's doctrine. In such a reconstruction scholars try to determine a set of principles or theses which, taken together, allow us to show why Plato says what he does about Forms, souls, and other metaphysical items.

Scholars have delved deep into the text of the dialogues and, with help from Aristotle, have pulled out what has come to be known as Plato's Theory of Forms. Distilling the ambiguity of the dialogue form into a proper philosophical doctrine, they endeavour in a task properly suited to Plato but which he unfortunately neglected (perhaps, one can only suppose, due to a strange sense of humour or because of some arbitrary whim). However, this exegetical endeavour is far from unproblematic. Silverman issues the following cautionary note: 'In the attempt to make more precise what Plato is after, one risks attributing to Plato *notions that are either not his or not as well developed in Plato as scholars would hope*' [my emphasis]. Plato left behind no philosophical prose, thus Plato did not hand down for posterity a theory or doctrine of Forms.

Turning to the dialogues, we certainly become acquainted with forms that are indeed perfect, timeless and changeless. A form (*eidos, idea*) is the one essential being over the many instantiations or particulars we encounter in our daily lives – for example, not this or that beautiful thing but beauty itself; and, beyond a shadow of a doubt, they are existents – the most real of all existents. This much we know from Plato, but there is not a single suggestion in any of the dialogues that we must evict these Forms from this world to live in some extra-terrestrial space beyond it. It is extremely difficult for realist, down-to-earth, thinking to contemplate existence as anything other than corporeal or somatic embodiment and this presents a problem: Platonic forms are also thought of as embodied, as having a certain 'physical' presence. They become ghostly entities, whose peculiar nature banishes them to live in the unearthly Realm of Forms. But *Plato never mentions any realm or world of Forms in any of the dialogues*. On the other hand, we can read in the dialogues about how the forms have neither spatial nor temporal existence, indicating the impossibility of their being embodied in any way whatsoever. The Forms are not dimensional beings – not here, not anywhere.

However, this is not to deny them objective validity. The modern mind tends to think of things as existing either 'out there' separate from us or 'in here' in the mind; the former are objective whereas the latter are merely psychologically constituted. The forms are not things of the world (this one or any other) but things of the intellect and, as such, have an objective nature different to that of empirical objects; their status as objects of the intellect does not mean that they are simply 'made-up' by the mind. Intellectual objects, such as 'triangle', for example, can never be known without an intellect capable of comprehending them but this does not mean that we make up what a triangle is, i.e. a three-sided two-dimensional shape whose three angles always add up to 180 degrees. We cannot change what it is to be a triangle, nor would 'triangleness' disappear if there were no humans, or any other creature with the appropriate cognitive faculty around to acknowledge its existence. It is the same with all the forms. Neither the triangle itself nor justice itself exists 'out there' or 'in here';

these spatial metaphors become obsolete when dealing with objects of the intellect. An advanced cognitive capacity is necessary to grasp them, but they are more than mere constituents of the mind – neither the triangle itself nor justice itself can fail to be anything other than what it is.[15]

The forms (*eidoi*) are best thought of not as transcendent entities but as objects that can be accessed through the intellect or understanding. With our sophisticated thought processes we can look at beautiful things, for example, and realise that they all have something in common – beauty. We also realise that the form or character of beauty must be the same in all cases, otherwise we could not recognise beautiful things for what they are, as things of beauty; and, it is this beauty which gives beautiful things the nature that they have – in Platonic parlance, the form 'Beauty' is the one essential being over the many instantiations. Our capacity for reflective thought allows us to recognise that the form or character of beautiful things can itself become something to be grasped and understood; we can, that is, ask the Platonic question 'what is it to be this thing?' This reading may ground the flight of 'a winged soul meeting with truth in a place beyond the heavens' (Guthrie in Hadot, 2005, p 25) but it has the advantage of offering an extremely plausible way of understanding the Platonic project.

The forms are objects of the intellect whose nature is there to be uncovered by creatures with the appropriate cognitive faculties. Fortunately for us, we happen to be such creatures. Unfortunately (or so it seems to some) there does appear to be rather a lot of them

15. It may appear to some that I have introduced the idea that there are not only empirical objects but also objects of the intellect with very little argument, but the naturalist assumption that the only objects with any reality are those of an empirical nature is simply that – an assumption. If we think of an object as a unity, or the identification of the same thing, in all the different perceptions we have of that thing (for example, every time we look at the kitchen table – the table viewed in the morning, the evening, from the top, from underneath, etc, we look at the same thing, or object) then there is no reason to limit objects to the empirical realm, as the identification of this unity is possible beyond it; for example, we can identify that '2' as the same thing each and every time it is written as a symbol, or represented in some other way, and every time anything is presented to us as a pair.

– there are forms for physical objects such as 'tableness', proper-
ties such as 'redness', 'squareness', relational terms such as 'same-
ness', 'difference' (and, if we have a red square, for example, does
this mean we have two forms – redness and squareness, or do we
have an extra third form – 'red-squareness'?) – this list can go on
and on. With so many forms, it may be asked where exactly are we
supposed to begin our inquiry? However, within the myriad of
forms that can be known, there are some that summon our attention more than others. Unsurprisingly, Platonists are most interested in discovering the form or character of those things that
mean the most to us – love,[16] friendship,[17] beauty[18] and so on. It is
with these forms that we begin our search and, rightly so, for in
coming to know these forms we come to know ourselves better.

Platonic philosophy is the process of coming to know the
forms, those with the most relevance to our distinctly human
existence, but this knowledge is not something that can be found
out for us and simply passed on – 'The Truth' is not something
that exists 'out there' waiting to be discovered once and for all.
Central to the Platonic enterprise is dialogue, or dialectic – the
communal 'art of dialogue' (*dialectikê technê*). This rigorous, yet
amicable, philosophical inquiry strives towards knowledge of the
forms and an understanding of what these things are gradually
unfolds as the inquiry progresses.[19] Being told about the forms is
simply the first step, understanding and wisdom require more
time – meaning is simply not the kind of thing that can be handed

16. See *The Symposium*
17. See *The Lysis*
18. See *The Hippias Major*
19. Although rigorous, dialectic is not an aggressive or essentially combative activity. Platonic philosophy is not about winning the argument
'at all costs'. (If an Ancient Greek wished to know how to 'make the
weaker argument the stronger' or 'how to argue on both sides of a dispute', he went to a sophist not a Platonist. See, for example, *The Protagoras*
or *The Euthydemus*) In true dialectic, the interlocutors 'must answer in a
manner more gentle and proper to discussion' (*Meno* 75c-d). Socrates'
less than amicable treatment of the sophists in the dialogues bearing their
names e.g. *Protagoras* and *Gorgias*, on the other hand, is the result of
Socrates' fight against their disingenuous methods of argument.

over from one person to another. The forms under investigation can only begin to mean something to the searcher when his relationship to them grows in clarity; the more he devotes himself to dialogue, the clearer the forms become and the more his understanding is increased. Words that start out relatively empty of meaning become fuller and richer through engaging in dialectic. As the searchers discuss together the nature of the form of courage,[20] for example, what it is *to be* courageous is revealed with ever-greater clarity.

The searchers are not interested in discovering the true nature of every form, which would be impossible. The brevity of human existence precludes such a possibility, but more importantly the meaning of some forms can never be fully realised by human searchers. For example, while at times we may embody forms such as courage – we can be courageous, we can never embody the form 'batness' i.e. we can never be a bat. Thus, although we can know some things about 'batness' (we are rather clever monkeys after all) a full understanding of what it is to be a bat necessarily escapes us. Our ability to embody certain forms, and not others, imbues them with a significance that would be impossible otherwise. The forms under investigation are those that mean the most to us because these are the forms (or character) of the virtues central to our human existence. All things have certain virtues that make them an excellent example of what they are and we are no different, but, as humans, there are some virtues with more relevance to our existence than others, and it is the form or character of these virtues that are sought out through engaging in philosophical dialogue.

As the meaning of these forms develop in significance, the connotations of the search itself become clearer to the searchers, or philosophers. The forms under investigation are the virtues that make up human excellence or *aretê*. Through developing a deeper understanding of the forms relevant to our existence, which all exist under the governance of the good – 'for how can one claim that a particular [object, action or event] is just, beautiful, courageous etc, unless it is also, in actuality, good?'[21] – the searcher

---

20. See *The Laches*
21. Rowe, 2007, p 78

comes to understand what it means to live a good life, as a human being. The significance of these forms develops as the search progresses, thus exponentially increasing the importance of the search into the true nature of the forms. As understanding develops, the virtues of human existence become more meaningful for the philosopher, ensuring that his life, as a human being, also has more meaning for him. As the significance of the forms and their central role in living a good life develops, the philosopher feels compelled to embody these virtues in his life, for 'is it at all possible to admire something, and spend time with it, without wanting to imitate it?' (*Republic* 500c). The philosopher is transformed through his knowledge of the forms; his life continually increases in richness and meaning and becomes a living embodiment of the good life.

The modern Platonist does not try to deny his place in the natural order of things nor does he try to disown his simian heritage. What he objects to is the naturalist assumption that the only real objects are those with a physical or somatic existence. The lives of most creatures are made up entirely of singular and concurrent occasions, which occur within a purely physical horizon, but our remarkable cognitive capacities allow us to recognise a unity or identity in the things we encounter – be they tables or courageous acts. We can recognise, that is, that things have a certain form or character (*eidos*). Furthermore, we can recognise that certain kinds of things or events all share the same form or character; for example, all beautiful objects share the property of beauty (or they would not be beautiful). We can turn our highly evolved intellect away from the various instantiations sharing in this characteristic and direct our minds towards the form (*eidos*) itself as a thing to be known. A Platonic form is an object of the intellect, whose nature is there to be uncovered through the endeavours of these rather clever monkeys.

However, this is not some futile quest into a truth 'out there' waiting to be discovered, which we hope will explain the meaning of our existence. The forms themselves have little or no meaning without our investigative endeavours. The truth, or the meaning, of the forms can only become a reality for a searcher through engaging in the philosophical enterprise, with the communal art of dialogue at its core. Meanings do not exist 'out there' intact and ready to be put to use when discovered; rather, it is the process of creatively engaging with the forms through dialectic that gives them their meaning. However, this productive effort on our part does not mean that we create what these forms are. The form or character of these intellectual objects is not psychologically constituted nor is their nature dependant upon their being cognised by creatures of a suitable intellect. Forms cannot be anything other than what they are or they would fail to account for the presence of that form in their various instantiations; for example, triangles may vary in appearance – big, small, red, blue, equilateral, isosceles, painted, imagined – but they all must have three angles, which total 180 degrees, for them to count as triangles. Through dialectic, the truth or meaning of the forms progressively reveals itself to us, and it is through this process that the forms gain in meaning.

The Platonic journey from the cave begins when we turn away from the shadows on the wall, no longer satisfied with the 'ready to hand' truths and the opinions of others, whether these are the truths of Ancient Greece or those of the modern Western world. As the philosopher moves out from the cave, barren forms become richer and fuller in meaning as he engages in the quest into their true nature for himself. This is the message behind the allegory of the cave. A meaningful life is only possible when we can no longer live at ease with accepting the truths of others, contented with seeking pleasure in distractions. A meaningful life demands a re-orientation of our souls towards the forms that mean the most to us, with the form of the good guiding us in our search. As the search progresses into the true nature of these forms, we fill our life with meaning, and continuing along this road, we live the good life. This is the motivation behind the philosopher's love of wisdom. The searcher is transformed through his philosophical journey as he moves from a world of darkness to one of every increasing light. It is the search that makes his life meaningful and with every step his desire to continue the search grows ever stronger, as his life grows in a richness that would never be thought possible had he remained satisfied with staring at shadows on the wall.

Further Reading/watching

Allen, R. E., *Plato: Ion, Hippias Minor, Laches, Protagoras* (New Haven & London: Yale University Press, 1996

Armstrong, Karen, *The Case for God* [Ch 3: Reason], Random House, Toronto, 2009

Barrow, Robin, *Plato*, Continuum Publishing, London, 2006

Brecher, *Getting What You Want: A Critique of Liberal Morality*, Routledge Press, London and New York, 1998

Hadot, Pierre, *Philosophy as a Way of Life*, Blackwell Publishing, Oxford, 1995

Plato, *The Republic* [trans: T. Griffith], Cambridge University Press, Cambridge, 2008

Rowe, Christopher, *Plato and the Art of Philosophical Writing*, Cambridge University Press, Cambridge, 2007

Silverman, Allen 'Plato's Middle Period Metaphysics and Epistemology' at

http://plato.stanford.edu/entries/plato-metaphysics/ [accessed 30 August 2009]

'The Cave: An Adaptation of Plato's Allegory in Clay' at http://www.youtube.com/watch?v=69F7GhASOdM [animation which began lecture, accessed 12 September 2009]

CHAPTER THREE

The Consolation of Stoicism?

Ciaran McGlynn

Introduction

At first blush Stoicism seems like the ideal philosophy for a time of economic downturn. It conjures up images of stiff-upper-lips and dogged determination. To be 'stoical' is seen as manifesting a particularly admirable virtue. When times get tough, the tough are the stoical ones. But what is Stoicism? Is it, in fact, a philosophy that is uniquely appropriate to hard times? Or, is it an outmoded set of ancient beliefs which have had no relevance since the fall of the Roman Empire? Do Stoical beliefs constitute the type of mind-set that would be useful either during a recession or as a means of getting out of one?

In hard times people often seek consolation in over-arching theories that explain why things are not all that bad when viewed in a wider context – a context that extends beyond the physical experience of their lives. They are unlikely to find rival economic analyses consoling, but they do find more abstract standpoints such as those of religion or philosophy a source of comfort. If one's own particular tale of woe can be diminished by viewing it from the standpoint of eternity or some cosmic plan, then that relief, although it doesn't help pay the mortgage, is something that is welcomed.

In the absence of any strongly held religious beliefs – beliefs that looked outmoded or silly during the good times – comfort from some non-religious but encompassing worldview has often seemed the next best thing. When times are bad, Stoicism seems to be the right philosophy for the non faint-hearted. Its reputation is justified; many of the grimmest and most determined who were influenced by Stoicism were Roman generals who stoically con-quered new lands and pushed back barbarian hordes. The Emperor Marcus Aurelius could happily slaughter German tribes by day and sit in his tent in the evening composing Stoic inspired meditations.

Historical Origins

But who were the Stoics and what were their doctrines? The founder of the movement, Zeno (c. 334-262 BCE),[1] came to Athens from Citium in Cyprus in the late fourth century BCE. Initially, he was strongly attracted by the philosophy of the Cynics which, under its founder, Diogenes of Sinope (c. 400-325 BCE), had been the first of the new schools of philosophy that had emphasised the importance of the individual over the well-being of the community. The Cynics had advocated living in accordance with nature which, for them, meant a disregard for the norms and standards of society. Their name comes from the Greek word for dog, *kynos*, because of their reputation for living in a base manner unconcerned with public opinion. Diogenes and his followers believed that living in accordance with the baser aspects of our nature was the only way of achieving true happiness and fulfilment. Diogenes himself owned nothing more than a loincloth and lived in a tub or wine-jar. He, like his followers, would engage in behaviour that was often lewd and offensive. Zeno, however, seems to have become rapidly disenchanted with the Cynic lifestyle and soon set up his own school of philosophy, a school that did not endorse the colourful conduct of the Cynics. He too, as we shall see, advocated living in accordance with nature, but he saw this as living a rational life that would be in harmony with the rationality that he believed to be the motive force of the universe. Zeno conducted his lectures in a *stoa* (a covered and colonnaded walkway) in the Athenian market. Because of his habit of walking up and down this *stoa* talking to his students he, and his followers, became known as the Stoics.

Philosophies like Stoicism and Cynicism were indicative of a change that had taken place in the Greek mindset as a result of the conquests of Philip of Macedon (c. 382-336 BC) and his son Alexander the Great (356-323 BC), which had changed for ever the

---

1. Not to be confused with the much earlier Zeno who was famous for his paradoxes.

geo-political and, hence, social landscape of Greek life. These Macedonian kings had effectively destroyed the original political unit of Greek life, the city state or *polis*. For centuries the Greeks had lived in self-governing and ferociously independent cities. They were Athenians, or Spartans, or Thebans first and Greeks only secondly. As for the non-Greeks, they were simply referred to as the *barbaroi* – the barbarians. Plato (428-348 BCE) and Aristotle (384-322 BCE) philosophised in the context of the independent city state and assumed that an individual's identity would be taken from his *polis* and that the good of the *polis* took precedence over the good of the individual. In fact, for Plato and for Aristotle, the notion of the individual as an entity separate from his community would have seemed contrary to nature. The person without a community was virtually an outlaw, one who could not belong. The good of the soul, the opportunity to practise the virtues appropriate to a human being, necessitated the person being a member of a society. The model of the uncivilised person was Homer's depiction of the Cyclops: an individual who lives alone without feelings of kinship. But with the amalgamation of the city states into the Macedonian empire the old certainties came under threat. The sense of belonging, of purpose, and of having real influence in one's *polis*, was weakened when the Macedonians combined all the Greek states into a single province within a larger empire. The Macedonians themselves spoke a form of Greek that bordered on the barbaric and ruled as absolute monarchs without regard for any democratic customs of their subjects.

While this period of down-grading of the *polis* constituted hard times for the Greeks, it was also a period of excitement and adventure. Many Greeks followed Alexander's armies east and settled the new cities – far different from the old city states – that he established from Alexandria to Bactria. In the absence of an individual finding peace and contentment within the old framework, there arose a need for new ways of finding one's place and peace in the world. The period after the death of Alexander, known as the Hellenistic period, saw the rise of philosophical traditions (known as Hellenistic philosophy) that sought to reconcile people to the new situation and to thus achieve happiness. Besides the Stoics and the Cynics, the Epicureans and the Sceptics also sought to show people how they, as individuals, could achieve happiness. The word that is translated as 'happiness' is the Greek term *eudaemonia* which, literally translated, would mean something like 'blessed by a benevolent spirit'. In fact, it meant more than what is now meant by 'happiness', it meant to flourish as an individual. A key characteristic of all these Hellenistic philosophies is the emphasis on the individual rather than the community. In a world where the old communities no longer held the same importance, the individual found himself adrift in the world and happiness, or flourishing, was something that was to be achieved individually.

The Stoic Philosophy
While the Epicureans advocated the pursuit of pleasure and the Cynics life in accordance with our animal instincts as means for achieving happiness, the Stoics proposed that we would only be happy if we recognised that the world was governed by a rational fate and that we yield to its inexorable demands. This philosophy of obeying the dictates of fate became very popular in the Hellenistic world in the third and second centuries BC and became equally popular in the Roman world from the second century BC up until at least the time of the Christian domination of the empire in the later fourth century AD. Stoicism tended not to be very speculative and concentrated more on practical means of achieving harmony with one's lot in the world. This practical aspect proved very popular with Roman statesmen and soldiers who, unlike the Greeks, were not over-fond of abstract ideas. Stoicism's popularity, especially among the educated Roman classes, only waned when Christianity (which Stoicism had influenced, especially through the writings of Saint Paul) became the dominant religion of the empire and sought to eradicate all rival systems of belief.

The central tenet of Stoicism is the view that human beings are directed by fate. Their philosophy thus starts from the human condition, and what struck Zeno about this condition is that human beings do not have any say over how life will turn out. For the Stoics, 'fate leads the willing man, the unwilling man it drags'. They likened the individual person to a dog that is tied to a cart. The dog can either choose to go with cart or it can pull against it. Either way it is going where the cart is going, but life will be much easier if it dutifully trots along behind. But determinism was not, for Zeno, a means of avoiding one's responsibilities. A story is told of how a slave of Zeno's was caught stealing and tried to avoid punishment by claiming that he was fated to steal, to which Zeno replied that he was thus also fated to be beaten. The Roman Stoic philosopher and ex-slave, Epictetus, used the simile later made famous by Shakespeare in *As You Like It*[2] that we are like actors on a stage. Someone else writes our parts, we can only play our role well or poorly.[3] Happiness, or flourishing as an individual, is learning to accept what fate decrees. The ability to accept one's fate is what the Stoics meant by living in accordance with nature. But this life in harmony with nature is very different from the Cynic origin of the notion. For the Cynics the happy person lived in a primitive and instinctive way, but for the Stoics happiness required the use of reason which dictates that we harmonise our thoughts and our goals with the rational order of the universe. To do that, we must understand the universe and that entails possession of knowledge. We must study the world to see how best we can live in it; the natural processes of the world reflect the rational mind – the fate that guided all of reality. To live rationally, that is, to live in accordance with nature, is to be virtuous.

There were a number of virtues which the Stoics saw as being of particular importance; to possess any one of these implied the possession of them all. The first is encapsulated in the multipurpose Greek term *phronesis* which is usually translated as 'prudence' or 'practical wisdom', although possibly better rendered as 'moral insight'.[4] This is the practical ability to make rational

---

2. Act II, Scene VII

3. Epictetus, *Encheiridion*, Section 17, in Michael L. Morgan, *Classics of Moral and Political Theory*, (Indianapolis, Hackett, 1992), p 430

4. The historian of philosophy, Frederick Copleston, translates it as 'moral insight'. See Frederick Copleston, *A History of Philosophy*, (New York, Image Books, 1962) Vol I, Part II, p 141

moral decisions. Also crucial to the Stoic ideal of the virtuous character is the possession of courage. The ability to face one's fate with resilience and to be unflinching in doing one's duty was central to the Stoic notion of character. It is hardly surprising that Stoicism has, since Roman times, been a particularly attractive philosophy for military men. Following on from courage, the Stoics emphasised the virtue of self-control. The Stoics taught the necessity of not yielding to the passions. Finally, one must also display the virtue of justice. In fact, to have *phronesis* was, *ipso facto*, to possess and display all the other virtues. There was disagreement between the earlier and later Stoics as to whether the Stoic character was actually achievable or whether it was merely aspirational. For the Stoics, to be wise was to practise or, at least, seek to practise, the virtues.

The great enemy to achieving a virtuous character was the lure of the passions. The Stoics' rivals, the Epicureans, maintained that the passions, in that they affected the all-important experience of pleasure, were the wellspring of human action. The Stoics saw the emotions or passions as a distraction from the pursuit of a rational life. It was passions such as fear of our own deaths or grief at the deaths of others, that prevented us from calmly and rationally accepting what fate had in store for us. All emotions like pleasure, desire and fear, are irrational. The rational acceptance of what life has in store for us, without complaint and without sorrow, is what makes Stoicism seem like the best philosophy for hard times. If we can accept that the material things we possess can go as easily, or more easily, than they came then we are less likely to be made unhappy at their loss. In fact, we are unlikely to want such things in the first place as their possession will be a matter of indifference to us. Similarly, if we can calmly accept that all those whom we love, and we ourselves, will pass away, we are less likely to feel grief at the death of loved ones or to fear our own demise.

A freedom from such emotions would lead a person to a state of *ataraxia*, a condition of being calm and unperturbed. This notion of *ataraxia* was common to the Stoics, the Epicureans, and the Sceptics. The idea was that happiness (*eudaemonia*) is something subjective and that it is better to be inwardly calm and free from anxiety than to be immensely wealthy and be in a state of apprehension. The Roman Stoic Epictetus maintained that: 'It is better to die of hunger with distress and fear gone than to live upset in the midst of plenty.'[5] But, as we have seen, this tranquillity of mind comes at a price. We must inure ourselves to the misfortunes, sickness, and death of ourselves and those we love. To the Stoics this was a small price to pay for the overwhelming benefit such inner calmness would bring. Nothing external would ever touch us; nothing would ever make us unhappy. But, one wonders, would such inner peace really compensate us for the lack of the intense emotional experiences that seem to be the essence of happiness? Material goods may come or go, and their coming or going may make us happy or sad, but the truly memorable high points of our lives seem to be associated with emotional experiences. What make these experiences memorable are the accompanying passions – passions which are downplayed in Stoic philosophy.

Stoicism grew out of the feeling of alienation many Greeks felt in a society that had undergone great change in which the old certainties and securities had been weakened. In the absence of strong communal bonds people are left with a society of individuals. It is this individualism that Stoicism not only caters for, but in effect encourages. Happiness, fulfilment and identity, is no longer sought within the community, it is now achieved (if it is achieved) by the individual. We live and die alone. The best we can do is to inoculate ourselves from the external sufferings and misfortunes of others. We see other individuals unhappy, but we do not let their unhappiness disturb our tranquillity. Our attitude to others is not guided by compassion; what regulates how we conduct ourselves in society is dictated by the notion of duty. This idea was especially embraced by the Romans. We must do our duty – this is the rational thing to do. Just as the rationality of the universe is observed through the laws of nature, so too human action is rationally guided by moral laws. We must abide by these laws and, above all, perform what is required of us without hesitation or fear.

The notion of rational behaviour harmonising with some cosmic plan made sense to the Stoics in the context of their belief that the

5. Epictetus, *Encheiridion*, Section 12, in Michael L. Morgan, op. cit. p 429

universe was permeated by a rational soul or god which they saw as fate. Not being primarily metaphysicians, they borrowed their metaphysical beliefs about the nature of the universe from the Pre-Socratic philosopher Heraclitus. Heraclitus had maintained that there is a universal rationale, or *logos*, that penetrates and guides the whole world. Furthermore, the universe's basic constituent was fire which comprised all that there is, including human souls. The universal reason was also constituted by fire. The Stoics adopted Heraclitus's metaphysics but elaborated upon it and equated universal reason with fate. For the Stoics their universal reason was composed of the same type of material, *pneuma*, as human souls. The cosmos was a living being and this being's soul was universal reason. When we reason correctly we are harmonising with, or participating in, this universal rational soul. Although the Stoics used the language of god and souls they did not believe in a transcendent reality. They adopted, without much critical questioning, a materialist metaphysics which committed them to the belief that everything, including god and souls, was composed of physical stuff. The basic physical stuff for the Stoics were the four elements of earth, air, fire, and water. *Pneuma*, the material that comprised the spiritual component of the universe, was composed of air and fire. It pervaded the entire universe and not only constituted those aspects of the universe that could think and reason, it also determined the nature of every single thing. The things in the universe are what they are because of the inherent *pneuma* within them. Like modern scientific materialists, the Stoics tried to explain too much with too little.[6] But then, metaphysical speculation was not really what interested them. As we have seen, they were not especially abstract thinkers. Their point of departure was ethical, not metaphysical. However,

---

6. Many contemporary scientists, such as Richard Dawkins, adopt, like the Stoics, the metaphysical standpoint of materialism. Such scientists often reject any notion of metaphysics; but rejection of belief in metaphysical speculation is no guard against holding a metaphysical position. They, again like the Stoics, try to explain all of nature, including human nature, from the resources of the current physical theories of the universe.

while not particularly interested in metaphysical speculation, by the fact that they held a worldview they could not escape holding a metaphysical position – another such position they adopted was determinism. What impressed itself on Zeno and his followers was the apparent fact that the events of the world, including our actions, are determined. Things will happen in accordance with the general cosmic unfolding and cannot be altered. All we can do is learn to go along with a good grace.

They disagreed among themselves over traditional beliefs regarding the continuation of the soul after death and the existence of the gods. Some maintained that the gods of the Greek pantheon were merely symbolic of various aspects of universal reason. Some, such as Cleanthes (331-232 BCE) believed that all souls survived death while Chrysippus (280-207 BCE) believed that only the souls of the wise would not be annihilated. However, this personal survival could hardly be called immortality, as all the Stoics agreed that every soul, along with the cosmos, would eventually be consumed by one of the periodic conflagrations that engulfed all of reality. This notion of cyclical destruction, usually by fire, from which phoenix-like a new cosmos would arise, was a common belief among the Greeks.

Contemporary Relevance

Although some of the Stoic beliefs, such as universal conflagration, do not find strong resonance within mainstream modern culture, many other aspects of their worldview do have similarities to the contemporary outlook of the western world. The Stoic materialist aspect would be one which many secular westerners might sympathise with in broad outline if not in the detail of their outmoded physics. The Stoics' materialism, unlike that of their Epicurean contemporaries, did not necessarily commit them to determinism. But, for reasons which were apparently not grounded in metaphysical presuppositions, they did adopt a deterministic view of the world. Their analysis of the human condition led them to see every person's life as being dominated by fate (with the inconsistent exception of our ability to choose freely how we should react to our fated condition). But while much of contemporary

European society could be characterised as being both secular and materialist (in both its metaphysical and economic senses) it is not fatalistic. Materialist theories, such as the atomism of Epicurus and pre-quantum physics, seem to be committed to a deterministic worldview. This deterministic view of the universe is vividly seen in the thought experiment of the French mathematician Pierre de Laplace's notion of a being that could know all that had happened or would happen.[7] If, as Laplace's experiment assumes, the world is wholly material and operates according to rigid laws like some giant machine, then it seems plausible that every event is predictable. Such an omniscient being – Laplace's demon – who can not only predict but also retrodict all future and past states of the world from a perfect knowledge of the laws and conditions of any present state, makes sense from a materialist outlook. Although post-quantum physicists are a lot charier about postulating future necessity, many other scientists and science-worshippers seem to be of the view that we live in a determined universe. There is something of a paradox here; while the underpinning science of the western world is materialist and deterministic, the people of the west are among the least fatalistic societies that have ever existed. In recorded history we encounter no other cultures that have been as non-fatalistic, innovative, and reluctant to accept the *status quo* as those societies that constitute western civilisation.

The impersonal nature of God is another Stoic belief that has a contemporary resonance. Among seculars, of course, there is no room for a God, personal or otherwise. But even among many religious believers in the west, God, thanks to the ever-growing explanatory power of science, is increasingly seen as a remote figure who does not take a personal hand in conducting the affairs of the world. Like the Stoics many in the west see prayer as inefficacious. Likewise, there would be sympathy with the Stoical and general Hellenistic philosophical view of the powerlessness of the individual in the face of the impersonal forces of nature and of global society. We live in super-states that are themselves compo-

---

7. Pierre de Laplace (1749-1827) put forward this view of an omniscient 'intellect' in *A Philosophical Essay on Probabilities* (1825)

nents of larger international combinations and in which the individual's lack of power and influence is pronounced. In fact, this very individualism is another feature that contemporary life has in common with the Stoic worldview. At no other time in history, not even in the era that saw the rise of Stoicism, were people so much condemned to individualism as in modern western society. Small nuclear families, and the de-emphasising of familial and emotional bonds has created societies in which more people live alone without communal roots or ties than in any other time.

All these correlations make Stoicism seem like the right kind of philosophy for a period of hardship and uncertainty. In fact, if we want to see a model that comes close to the Stoic ideal of how one should live we need only look at the depiction of the hero of popular culture. The James Bonds, Jason Bournes, and Jack Bauers of this world display the traits that the Stoics aspired to. They manifest bravery, control of emotions, a strong sense of duty, a lack of sentiment, and a resilience in the face of the death or illness of loved-ones.

Finally, the Stoic ideal that we must understand the world in order to use the knowledge as a guide to behaviour also has a strong resonance today. The proliferation of sciences and the cult of the expert, speak of a society that craves knowledge as a guide to conduct. Statistics have become the new god, with the ability to cite such data as a necessary prerequisite for any proposal to be taken seriously. Non-statistical disciplines are seen as vague and woolly and are designated as 'arts'. But, as serious guides to conduct, be it on how to teach students or whether to give money to poor nations, it is assumed that we first need to master the relevant scientific data, and this knowledge is generally enshrined in statistics. While the possession and use of such knowledge as a guide to behaviour seems obvious to the western mind, it is not so obvious to members of non-western cultures. In such cultures, scientific knowledge, statistical or otherwise, often takes second place to tradition or faith, and the notion that observation of the physical world could be a guide to spiritual wellbeing would seem odd.

Some Reservations on Stoicism

In spite of Stoicism's resonance with some aspects of the modern mindset, the philosophy does have some obvious demerits. First, the injunction 'live in accordance with nature' does not tell us much about what we should or should not do. It seems to be an unwarranted assumption that there is some rational course of action which, if followed, corresponds with the rationality of fate. As we all know, there are often many competing and equally rational courses of action open to us; how do we decide between them? Secondly, to say 'follow the laws of nature' seems redundant when we have no choice but to do so. The Stoic will respond that we can choose how we accept the dictates of fate. Like the dog, we might be dragged along behind the cart, but at least we can choose how we mentally respond to this compulsion. We can stoically accept it, or we can struggle against it and hence have a very unhappy life. However, this response leads on to a third criticism: The Stoics, by claiming that we can choose how to respond to the relentless dictates of nature, are contravening their own fatalistic or deterministic philosophy. If we are free to choose our own mental states then the world, or at least part of the world, is not determined; fate is not as implacable and all-encompassing as it had been thought. The Stoics, of course, were aware of this shortcoming in their philosophy and comprehensively tied themselves in knots trying to fit the square peg of human mental freedom into the round hole of universal determinism. Their failure is being repeated today with equally enthusiastic materialists who try to formulate a view of the world that essentially denies the common human experience of freedom. It is, again, a case of materialists trying to do too much with too little.[8]

8. For example, philosophers like Daniel Dennett, who are impressed by the success of the scientific materialist model of the world, try to explain all phenomena, including the phenomenon of consciousness, in terms of a third person materialist ontology. To many philosophers, the resources of materialism are just too poor to do justice to the rich and complex phenomenon that is consciousness. Likewise, being impressed – or oppressed – by a materialist metaphysics, Dennett is willing to embrace the apparently inevitable doctrine of determinism. We only believe we are free because of our limited capacities to grasp the whole picture.

So, is Stoicism a consolation in a time of recession? Should we advocate the Stoic virtues of moral insight, courage, self control, and a sense of justice to those who are suffering economic misfortune? Evidently, the ability to face resolutely whatever happens is useful during tough times. But to tell someone that they should accept misfortune because it is inevitable within the cosmic scheme of things is probably not the kind of justification that will motivate them. However, such solace did seem to motivate many in the past; think of Romans who apparently found solace in knowing that they must perform their duties and face the inevitable merely because it was inevitable and doing their duty was the right thing to do. But why, in a modern western liberal democracy, would such a justification not seem as plausible as it did two millennia ago? The answer is that the western mindset is radically different from its ancient forbear. Not the least of the reasons for this difference is the domination for so many centuries of the western worldview by Christianity. Christianity, on the whole, tends to be an optimistic (i.e. non-deterministic) religion with the live hope of universal salvation. The fact that western culture was saturated with Christian optimism (about the non-determined nature of the future) in no small part helped to form a forward-looking civilisation whose members deeply believed that they could change their lot on earth. Although some Christian philosophers and theologians got themselves tied in knots (as elaborate as those of the Stoics) over the question of determinism stemming from God's foreknowledge of events, most ordinary people emphasised the other aspect of Christianity – its commitment to human freedom. This non-fatalistic attitude played a large part in the Scientific Revolution in the seventeenth century and the Enlightenment and Industrial Revolutions of the eighteenth and nineteenth centuries.[9] This frame of mind has produced a civilisation that is less fatalistic than any other society

9. Marx had claimed that the masses of the western industrial nations were being tranquilised by religion into not seeing the true nature of their servitude. Thankfully, the non-fatalistic western society that Christianity helped to create enabled its members to shrug-off the deterministic doctrine of dialectical materialism and thus avoid the fatal waff of the Marxist opiate.

for which we have records. While fatalistic societies tend not to be progressive (in terms of social, economic, scientific, and techno-logical innovation), a hallmark of advanced industrial societies is that they contain creative individuals who do not accept the *status quo*. The Stoic attitude of accepting what is inevitable could lead to passivity and resignation. A truly Stoical society would probably be one in which the members were reluctant to initiate change and would only 'stoically' accept such change if it were imposed from without.

A further demerit of a wholehearted Stoicism is that it would tend to de-emphasise the emotions and lead to an even more un-feeling society. The dispassionate acceptance of life's ups and downs could lead to a non-community of stultified and damaged individuals. The idea of emotional detachment is the greatest weakness of Stoicism and an aspect which makes it a singularly inappropriate philosophy for a time of recession. In an era when more people than ever are in need of kindness, consideration, and material help, we need more, not less, compassion. The ability to accept stoically the suffering of others further weakens the bonds of a society and lessens the prospects for the type of co-operation that would mitigate the worst excesses of economic hardship and create the innovative solutions to return us to prosperity.

Not only could the Stoic ideal lead to a fracturing of society, the experiences that make us truly happy are the very emotions that the Stoics downplay. The Stoic form of happiness, freedom from anxiety, appears to be at the cost of the things that genuinely bring us contentment: the presence of loved ones and the fulfilment we get from emotional experience. Such experiences constitute the memorable and happy episodes of our lives: falling in love, the birth of a child, exotic travels, or whatever, are the events that we mark as our positive biographical milestones. But our lives also have negative milestones and these events, with their accompany-ing emotions, are also part of our individual stories and make us the people we are. To downplay our emotions and become as cold and as unaffected as possible by the fate of others seems to do damage to our very humanity. There are, to be sure, elements of stoicism in contemporary society, but they are generally not the elements we wish to nurture. Coldness, remoteness, and resignation, are probably not the traits that will make us happy in a time of recession – nor will they be the attributes that get us out of the recession. Stoicism may work for a society of dulled sensitivities, a society in which its members could be defined in terms of a few abstract qualities, such as those that depict an individual as purely an economic unit. But people are more complex than any set of abstractions can encompass, and there are many other philosophies to which a person can turn for consolation.

Some Introductory Texts on Stoicism

Campbell, R., 1969, *Seneca: Letters From A Stoic*, Harmondsworth, Penguin.

Inwood, B., 2003, *The Cambridge Companion To Stoicism*, Cambridge, CUP.

Inwood, B., and L. P. Gerson, 1988, *Hellenistic Philosophy: Introductory Readings*, Indianapolis, Hackett.

Inwood, B., and L. P. Gerson, 2008, *The Stoics Reader: Selected Writings and Testimonia*, Indianapolis, Hackett.

Irvine, W. B., 2009, *A Guide To The Good Life: The Ancient Art of Stoic Joy*, Oxford, OUP.

Long, A. A., 1986, *Hellenistic Philosophy: Stoics, Epicureans, Sceptics*, London, Duckworth.

CHAPTER FOUR

Recognising the Limits:
A Philosophical Critique of Consumerism

Brendan O'Byrne

The title 'The Consolations of Philosophy: Reflections for an economic downturn' suggests that philosophy might have some consolatory support to offer in a time of recession. However, in this contribution I want to mount a philosophical criticism of the kinds of beliefs and behaviour that leads to recessions as well as to growth periods in an advanced capitalist society. The so-called 'Boom and Bust' cycle is an ineradicable feature of a mass consumerist economy, and a systemic feature which has huge personal and social costs as well as the supposed benefits. I want to suggest that philosophy is *most* needed in times of economic growth. It is when the possibility of giving oneself over to self-indulgence looms largest, that philosophy is most needed. Looking at philosophy as a possible source of consolation in recession times is, in my view, getting things backwards.

I want to consider consumerism as an ethical claim, criticise it from a number of perspectives, and then briefly propose an alternative suggested by traditional philosophy. As the emphasis in this essay is ethical rather than socio-political the main focus here will be on the individual. Some reference to sociological, historical and political factors will be unavoidable but I will confine the discussion, as much as possible, to the individual and the kind of lifestyles that are promoted as desirable and even normative.

Let me begin with some basic concepts and loose definitions. What is a recession? Recession is simply a slow-down in economic activity. Economists have no universally agreed definition of when an economy can be described as in recession. However, there are some common indicators; a period when GDP drops for two consecutive quarters is generally agreed to be recessionary but some economists would add that a 1.5% increase in unemployment should also be included in any definition. Recession should really be understood in relation to its opposite, growth. Growth is an increase in economic activity. Growth is held to be a good thing and this is indeed a sacred dogma that anyone who wishes to make progress in public life must regularly affirm. On the other hand, recession is a very bad thing, to be avoided at all costs. Depression – a severe and sustained recession – is deemed the worst evil so much so that the very word tends to be avoided. We even hear media economists using the term 'the D-Word' in a way that recalls the superstitious avoidance of mentioning the devil in times gone by! It is an article of faith that continuous expansion of economic activity is supremely desirable, and a static economy is a bad thing. All of this is proclaimed without any real attempt at rationally justifying it, for in the context of a finite planet, whatever other objections might be raised, this is a physically unsustainable vision. In the first part of this essay I want to connect the economic phenomenon of growth to the psychological phenomena of the appetites and the passions, trace the development of consumerism for the masses, and then I will interpret these developments in terms of an implied ethical theory. I will conclude by outlining some classic philosophical responses to the appetites which include the cultivation of the virtues and the practice of self-discipline (*askesis*).

Contemporary western liberal democratic capitalist society is organised in such a way as to maximise the supply of goods and services to the greatest number. There is in principle no limitation to the amount of such goods that an individual can acquire, other than those imposed by the size of their purse. Likewise, there is no limit to the amount of money an individual can pursue or possess nor are there restrictions, save those imposed by law, on what the individual may do with the money they have acquired; they are permitted to buy a Ferrari but not a slave.

In the liberal bourgeois polity that first arises in the 17th century, political considerations have steadily become subordinated to economic imperatives. One of the basic tenets of classical liberalism is the primacy of the private sphere – civil society – over the public sphere – the polity – and possessive individualism. The latter is the view that we are each of us the sole proprietors of our talents and skills, which should be bought and sold in the market because we owe each other nothing. This view is based on the more basic belief that we are innately selfish.[1] This is a central feature of the consensus that extends across the spectrum of mainstream political parties in the western world today. Those who do not accept this formula – that economic arguments trump nearly all other considerations – are outside of this consensus and are considered extremists, fringe elements or just irrelevant.

The thesis that I will pursue and, hopefully justify, is this: the current reigning paradigm of human happiness defined here as consumerism is false. Not only is it false, it is destructive of both individuals, the societies in which it is dominant, and if left unchecked, ultimately, of the world itself. The crux of the argument is that consumerism cannot lead to happiness; thus it would follow that consumerism is intrinsically unable to meet its own utilitarian criterion of success: bringing the greatest happiness to the greatest number. The notion of utility underlying this holds that use values are the governing principles of action. Utilitarianism is a Consequentialist ethical theory. Consequentialism holds that 'all actions are right or wrong in virtue of the value of their consequences' whereas non-consequentialism is the view that 'some acts are right or wrong whatever the consequences.' Hedonism holds that 'pleasure is the good' and if we only ever pursue the good, as it seems to us at least, then 'pleasure is the only possible object of desire or pursuit' therefore, normatively, 'pleasure is what we ought to desire or pursue'. The Utilitarian principle holds that when faced with a choice we should only act in such a way as to contribute to the 'the greatest happiness for the greatest number'.[2] In addition, questions of moral character and psychology are not particularly relevant to the moral evaluation of acts under this view.

1. The concept of 'possessive individualism' was formulated by C. B. Macpherson in his book *The Political Theory of Possessive Individualism: From Hobbes to Locke*, Oxford: Clarendon Press, 1962
2. See the entries for 'Consequentialism', 'Hedonism', and 'Utilitarianism' from Ted Honderich (ed) *The Oxford Companion to Philosophy*, Oxford University Press, 1995

Now, I would claim that consumerism cannot bring the greatest happiness to even a single individual, let alone the greatest number. Instead we need to rethink our notions of the happy life in ways that are personally fulfilling and collectively sustainable.

The rejection of consumerism should not be understood as denying that we must consume things in order to live, nor is it to say that what we term goods and services are not good, nor is it even to deny that luxury goods and services can not be desirable.[3] I am simply denying that consumerism as a lifestyle choice can ever lead to happiness. In other words, western consumer societies are based on a set of premises and promises that ultimately cannot be delivered upon.

So what is consumerism? What does it mean philosophically? The simple lexical definition offered by the *Oxford English Dictionary* defines it as 'a doctrine advocating a continual increase in the consumption of goods as a basis for a sound economy' and an '(excessive) emphasis on or preoccupation with the acquisition of consumer goods.' From an ethical point of view, consumerism amounts to the claim that consumption of goods and services will lead to happiness. I would add that consumerism, in our significant sense, concerns the acquisition of goods and services that are not strictly necessary, for instance, a CD collection, cosmetics, or a skiing holiday. Any belief or set of inter-related beliefs that purport to answer the question of human happiness is by definition an ethical theory or is at least a claim or set of claims that can be formalised as a theory.

Mass consumerism is a relatively new phenomenon but its underpinnings are very old. It is a version of ethical hedonism and its basic premise is that pleasure is the only intrinsic good. Put it another way, the term good *means* pleasant or pleasurable. Also,

---

3. I say 'can not' rather than 'are not' for this latter would suggest that things classed as goods are intrinsically desirable. Context and inculturation are important factors – a shovel and a sack of seeds would be far more desirable than a Ferrari to a man stranded on a desert island, even though he would likely prefer the car back in civilisation. A well-made blow-pipe would be more desirable to a New Guinea Highlander than a high speed internet connection. Examples such as these render the notion of the intrinsic desirability of external and contingent goods problematic.

consumerism as a mass phenomenon implies utilitarianism, which is why I distinguish between consumerism as such, which has always been a feature of civilised societies, and mass consumerism, which is relatively recent. The extension of consumerism to the masses satisfies both hedonic and utilitarian ethical principles.

Part of the success of my thesis rests on the assumption that all human beings pursue happiness as the ultimate aim of life and therefore happiness is pursued for its own sake. If this is accepted then any disputes will revolve around definitions of happiness. It would follow that if we are aiming at happiness then happiness is our good and all those different things we call good would be good by derivation. Their goodness would consist in their being instrumental in attaining our ultimate end. This is not to exclude other classes of things which might be good for their own sake, like listening to music.

Returning to the basic tenet of ethical hedonism and combining this with my remarks about happiness, we can set out a provisional formula as follows: if pleasure is the good, then the good life, i.e. happiness, is achieved through the maximisation of pleasure and, conversely, the minimisation of pain. We are left with this set of premises. The good life is a life of pleasure, and on combining this with the utilitarian principle, then consumerism consists of the maximisation of the good (i.e. pleasure) for the greatest number.

One curious feature about consumerism as hedonic utilitarianism is its lack of pedigree in the philosophical tradition. It dates back no further than the late 18th century as exemplified by Jeremy Bentham (1748-1832), its best known exponent. Traditionally though, ethical hedonism was associated with Epicureanism, a radical materialist philosophy founded in late 4th-century BCE Athens which held that the ultimate aim of life should be a state of tranquil detachment (*ataraxia*), that is, happiness (*eudaimonia*) consisted in attaining this state. This was to be achieved, in part, through a withdrawal from the stresses and strains of public life and the maximisation of pleasure and the minimisation of pain. However, here we find a very different conception of hedonism than the one underlying mass consumerism. Epicurus' pleasure is probably best understood negatively, simply as absence or elimination of pain. The example of thirst should suffice to illustrate the bare essentials of his hedonic theory. Thirst is a form of pain, quenching it a form of pleasure. The maximal pleasurable state is finally achieved when thirst is eliminated through quenching. At this point continuing to drink could very well turn into pain. Pleasure, on this understanding, is vital for the desired state of *ataraxia*. If we are hungry or thirsty we are agitated and distressed, the opposite of tranquil and untroubled. Pleasure as equilibrium is a necessary condition for attaining *ataraxia*. Epicurus is also adamant that we avoid unnecessary desires so as not to become dependent on unnecessary pleasures. But consumerism is premised on the cultivation of desire for unnecessary things and it is this which radically marks it off from Epicurean hedonism. It is therefore beyond question that Epicurus would have condemned consumerism precisely because it involves the excitation of the appetites and the stimulation of new and unnecessary desires. Let us take a brief look at how and why consumerism entails the stimulation of unnecessary desires through a brief historical excursus.

The advent of mass consumerism came about largely through a crisis in capitalism caused by over-production capacity, in turn, brought about through the development of new technologies and efficiency techniques in industrial production. As Richard Robbins in his book *Global Problems and the Culture of Capitalism* puts it:

> [T]he consumer revolution of the late nineteenth and early twentieth centuries was caused in large part by a crisis in production; new technologies had resulted in production of more goods, but there were not enough people to buy them. Since production is such an essential part of the culture of capitalism, society quickly adapted to the crisis by convincing people to buy things, by altering basic institutions and even generating a new ideology of pleasure. The economic crisis of the late nineteenth century was solved, but at considerable expense to the environment in the additional waste that was created and resources that were consumed. (p 210)[4]

4. Richard Robbins, *Global Problems and the Culture of Capitalism*, Allyn and Bacon, 1999.

As long as there has been civilisation there has been consumerism but hitherto it had been confined to the relatively small circles of the wealthy and better off. Technology changed all this and with it came a requirement for a vast social engineering project to initiate the previously excluded masses into a lifestyle of unnecessary desire and consumption. People had to be trained to desire things they did not need, desire had to be aroused and cultivated if they were to be made avail of the newly plentiful goods. Robbins again:

> [There had to be a] change in spiritual and intellectual values from an emphasis on such values as thrift, modesty, and moderation, toward a value system that encouraged spending and ostentatious display. (p 21)

It should be noted that moderation is one of the classical virtues – *sophrosune* - therefore consumerism entails the substitution of vice for virtue. Paul Mazer, a prominent Wall St banker in the early 1920s, put it quite starkly:

> We must shift America from a needs to a desires culture. People must be trained to desire, to want new things even before the old had been entirely consumed. We must shape a new mentality in America. Man's desires must overshadow his needs. (quoted in the BBC documentary *Century of the Self*)[5]

This training of unnecessary desire amounts, in classical terms, to the exhortation to embrace vices like immoderation and envy. This latter is what is at stake in the trend towards ostentation mentioned by Robbins. It formed the centre piece of Thorstein Veblen's now classic study of consumerism, *The Theory of the Leisure Class* (1899) where he coined the now familiar term 'conspicuous consumption'.[6]

> It is true of dress in even a higher degree than of most other items of consumption, that people will undergo a very consid-

5. BBC TV, *Century of the Self, Part 1: Happiness Machines*. The series was first shown on BBC 4 between 29 April and 2 May 2002, 7pm-8pm
6. Thorstein Veblen, *The Theory of the Leisure Class*, Edited with an Introduction and Notes by Martha Banta, (Oxford World's Classics), Oxford, 2007

erable degree of privation in the comforts or the necessaries of life in order to afford what is considered a decent amount of wasteful consumption; so that it is by no means an uncommon occurrence, in an inclement climate, for people to go ill clad in order to appear well dressed. (p 111)

Good but cheap copies enable people to display the brand names of affluence and thereby project an image of themselves of being wealthier than they really are. Conspicuous consumption, or ostentatious display, is part of what is commonly referred to as 'keeping up with the Jones's'. Karl Marx rather perceptively saw this in terms of envy, another classic vice. Marx thought that envy was the real meaning of competition. As we all know competition is another one of those sacred dogmas of capitalism which is perpetually intoned by the punditry whenever economic issues come up for discussion in the public space.

Envy can provoke at least two responses; one is to try to match the envied one, the other is to deprive the envied one of whatever it is that is the object of envy, and ultimately level everyone down to the lowest common denominator: 'If I can't have it, you can't have it either.' This lies behind what Marx called 'crude communism'. This impulse of envy is provoked by the spectacle of wealth witnessed by the less wealthy and stimulates, as he says, 'the desire to reduce everything to a common level; so that this envy and levelling in fact constitutes the essence of competition. Crude communism is only the culmination of such envy and levelling-down on the basis of a preconceived minimum.'[7]

The extension of consumerism to the masses enabled the ruling group, which under capitalism is always the rich, to stultify the dangerous levelling impulse always lurking amongst the masses which were traditionally excluded from luxurious living. This was done by extending the possibility of a lifestyle of consumer acquisition to all classes in society. Instead of being outside looking in, the masses could be brought inside for a budget version of the high life. We can all fly abroad to holidays in the sun;

7. Karl Marx 'Private Property and Communism' in the *Economic and Philosophic Manuscripts of 1844* in David McLellan, *Karl Marx: Selected Writings,* Oxford University Press, 2000 (2nd ed)

the super rich have their own aircraft, the well off go first class, and the rest of us have the budget airlines. All this is only possible on the basis of massive industrial production capacity, the extension of efficiency techniques to social management, and last, but not least, the extension of credit facilities to the masses. This latter development begins in the form of the old purchase by instalment schemes, such that as early as 1920 most Americans had experimented with occasional instalment buying. Later on, ordinary people were encouraged to open bank accounts, avail of short-term loans, and be brought to a stage where they considered property purchase through long-term mortgaging to be quite normal. The most recent addition to this has been the mass extension of credit card facilities. Even up to relatively recently, these were the province of the better off segments of society, but now they have become the norm throughout. Mass consumerism requires considerable indebtedness as a norm if it is to work.

From this all too brief review of mass consumerism we can start to get a sense of why public discourse is saturated with the sacred dogmas of 'growth', 'competition' and 'consumer choice' etc. These things are presented as immutably set in stone and all sectors of the political spectrum must defer to them. The immense power of financial and industrial capital is sitting on everything, it controls all economic activity, it has corrupted the political process, saturated the culture with its exigencies such that they appear almost natural and it has seduced the masses with a steady supply of relatively cheap goods. It would not be an exaggeration to say that the world order has been thoroughly transformed to revolve around the imperatives of the mass consumer economy and its accompanying social forms. There seems to be only two ways in which this state of affairs could be altered: one way is as a result of nature itself imposing a terminal limit to endless growth – the oil dries up, other non-renewable resources are exhausted, and the environment kicks back. This is a likely end as envisaged by a growing number of people and when the collapse comes, it will cause a period of unprecedented global chaos. The other – and much more desirable – way out is through individual and personal transformation.

So far I have described something of the history of mass consumerism; how and why it arose. I have also indicated some of the ways in which it has effected a social and moral transformation and, important for present purposes, given a brief theoretical description of mass consumerism as hedonic utilitarianism. Now I want to turn to the philosophical critique of mass consumerism in order to demonstrate why it cannot but fail to fulfil the promise of human happiness that it offers. I will conclude by suggesting that the best lifestyle is one based on a more prudential attitude towards the acquisition of material goods, one which is genuinely sustainable, both personally and collectively, and which rests on a comprehensive revaluation of life aims along lines very different from those which are currently promoted.

One or two of the essays here have taken the view that philosophy is incapable of consolation – it's simply not within its purview and people should not look to it for such. There is a lot of truth in this view if by philosophy we understand it to refer to what generally goes in a modern university philosophy department. To make any real sense of philosophy as having consolatory potential, we need to return to the ancient schools and survey the situation there, particularly as the very notion of *consolatio philosophiae* emerges at the end of the ancient tradition in the person of Boethius (c. 480-524 CE). It would surely not be an exaggeration to say that an ancient school of philosophy more resembled something like a religious community than it would a modern philosophy department. If contemporary philosophers are almost entirely taken up with abstract and theoretical questions, the ancients were primarily concerned with the existential-transformative aim of philosophy. Philosophy is the method by which we address the question 'what is the good life for man?', but not for the sake of theoretical definitions, rather for the sake of practice. The student of philosophy was expected to be cultivating the cardinal virtues and philosophy was the means to the attainment of the supreme virtue, wisdom, hence the very term *philo-sophia* as love of wisdom. The love of wisdom is not a love of abstract theoretical learning for its own sake, but an active pursuit of the condition of being wise which, of course, involves theoretical knowledge.

The theoretical side to philosophy was pursued, ultimately, to provide explanatory justification for the ethical orientation of the particular school, its *hairesis*. This word is the root of the term 'heresy' and simply means 'choice' in Greek but which was then given a pejorative sense by the Christians. The ethical precepts of the school stood as a kind of answer, be it provisional or dogmatic, to the question: what is the good life?

According to Plato, Socrates experienced a life-change on the basis of an oracle that was delivered by the oracle of Apollo at Delphi in response to a question presented by one of Socrates' most ardent admirers, Chaerophon: 'Is there anyone wiser than Socrates?' The response was 'There is none wiser than Socrates.' (Plato, *Apology*, 21a) It was this which allegedly drove Socrates' inquiries in the public places of Athens in his search for an interpretation of this oracle which fitted in with his own sense of not knowing. Socrates was acutely conscious of his lack of knowledge of those things which he deemed as essential for wisdom. He believed that by interviewing all those with reputations for knowledge he could be brought closer to resolving the puzzle posed by the oracle. He eventually solved the puzzle when he came to the insight that unlike all those who thought they had knowledge, he had an acute sense of his own shortcomings in knowledge and it was precisely this insight which made him wiser than everyone else.

The Delphic command to know oneself (*gnothi sauton*) should best be understood as an address to the human as such rather than a personal command. The divine command to know oneself could only be fulfilled on the basis of an inquiry into the human essence: what is a human being? After all, how could one come to know a particular something without first knowing something about the class of thing to which it belongs? The search for self-knowledge revolves around the inquiry into what is a human being, or what it is to *be* a human being. Once we have some knowledge as to what a human being is in essence, we can come to know ourselves. This knowledge, let's call it a philosophical anthropology, serves as a kind of paradigm or criterion against which one can understand oneself.

The Delphic command to self-knowledge is tied into the driving question of ethical inquiry: what is the good life? The idea that there is an objective human nature that can in principle be identified and defined is one that has fallen into unpopularity in modern philosophy yet it was a view common to most of the ancients. Tied into this was the idea that we have a *telos* or end, a view sometimes described as functionalism. We may deny a determinable human essence and concomitant end but it seems to me undeniable that all human beings strive directly or indirectly for happiness. One would be tempted to say that every human being is a being so constituted as to seek its own end, which is to attain happiness or *eudaimonia* as the Greeks called it.[8] But even if we were to fall short of going that far and re-embracing functionalism (and there are good reasons not to), we might still agree that we all strive for happiness. On this understanding, the good life would be a life so arranged as to lead the individual to *eudaimonia* and we would need to include this in any ethical theorising we engage in. The key point here, on which everything else rests, is the claim that we all aim at happiness and that the good life is a life that will lead us towards happiness. It would follow from this that anything which conduces towards happiness would be good, and that which detracts or impedes, bad.

However, this is where the disputes start. What is happiness and what kind of life is best suited to attaining it? Our hedonist will say: pleasure is the good and anything that maximises pleasure is, by implication, good, and the opposite, bad. We have already seen that mass consumerism rests on this equation and adds utilitarianism as a theory of action designed to maximise the good for the greatest number. But we are disputing this formula; how do we proceed?

8. *Eudaimonia* is very difficult to translate satisfactorily into English or indeed any modern language. It consists of two words, the prefix *eu* - meaning well and *daimon* meaning something like a spirit or a very low-ranking divinity. The word literally means something like 'presided over by a beneficent spirit'; it is however the standard Greek term for happiness, or a life that works out well. Our expression 'blessed' might come close: 'he led a blessed life' but for present purposes I take happiness to denote 'a life that turns out well' over and against the relatively trivial sense of happiness as a feeling or mood.

There is such that could be said in criticism of the hedonic claim but I will confine myself to one powerful objection that goes back to the ancients. The objection runs as follows. Nearly everyone, if not everyone, would acknowledge that there is some meaning in talking about good and bad pleasures. For example, most would condemn the pleasure of the sadist in torturing people, or that of the cannibal in eating human flesh. These are deliberately extreme examples simply to make the point; if we are to talk about good or bad pleasures and agree that such talk is meaningful, then we have already separated pleasure and the good. They cannot be identical, unless one was to maintain the consistency of the equation no matter what, but this would lead to absurdity. We recognise that living without the ability to experience pain would be a bad thing because we would damage ourselves otherwise; we might not remove our hand from the fire, resulting in its destruction. Pain seems to be a good thing in an important sense. We must guard against identifying desirable with good and *vice versa*. Pain is undesirable but it is a good in that complex organisms rely on the capacity to experience pain for survival and to remain healthy. Once we gain agreement that there is a difference between pleasure and the good, then the hedonist's claim collapses; pleasure *cannot* be the good, if we simply agree that there are such things as bad pleasures.

If we can now claim that the equation of pleasure with the good cannot stand up, then we have destroyed one of the foundations of mass consumerism. However, this is not to say that pleasure does not have a legitimate position in any account of the good life, just that it cannot be equated with the good and therefore the life of pleasure cannot be a candidate for the good life, that is, a life that works out well.[9]

---

9. I would certainly want to criticise Utilitarianism as a form of Consequentialism on the grounds that it imposes impossible demands on people (to regard the good of the whole world as the object of action) and reduces to the question-begging and the ultimately, I would argue, amoral dictum: 'the end justifies the means.' Surely moral and ethical theories ought to have something to say about the qualities of actions themselves as well as the character of agents (persons) if they are to be truly moral.

If consumerism is not the means to a happy life, then what is? What would an alternative lifestyle look like in a society such as ours? In Plato's *Philebus* the argument revolves around precisely this issue. The candidates for the good life are pleasure and the life of the mind, but both are criticised by Socrates, who commends a mixed life: a life ruled by intellect but with a place for pleasure. It is important to emphasise that this is not to be understood as in any way comparable to David Hume's belief that the intellect is the slave of the passions, but rather on Plato's view it is the passions which must obey reason.[10] If the full story was to be told about the origins of modern consumerism, a detailed consideration of the views of people like Hume and others would play a central role. The 17th and 18th centuries saw the initial ground-laying of the kind of anthropological and ethico-political foundations of consumerism which also involved an overthrow of the older conceptions of man and the virtues. Instead of reason as the arbiter and source of norms for action, it was henceforth regarded as purely instrumental for securing the objects of our passions and desires. The kind of alternative I'm proposing would entail a rediscovery and retranslation of the traditional conceptions of the relations between reason and the passions such that the supreme value of a life of virtue would appear to be as natural as it did for pre-liberal consumer age people.

Individually it would require an acknowledgement that pleasure alone cannot fulfil the seemingly universal search for happiness, a corresponding acknowledgement that intellect can impose its order over the person, against Hume's claim to the contrary, and that this comprises the best possible life for us. We can confound Hume simply by citing the example of a great many people who have freed themselves from the snares of the most demanding and cruel passions of which they were previously enslaved. I'm thinking here of people who have overcome addictions. Addicts who have followed the path to liberation from these

---

10. Hume famously declared 'Reason is, and ought only to be the slave of the passions, and can never pretend to any other office than to serve and obey them.' The Platonic view completely rejects and reverses this formulation.

fierce passions have often followed programmes which on close examination contain many features familiar to the students of ancient and pre-modern philosophy; the self-knowledge theme employing a dialectical procedure for self-examination, acknowledgement of a power greater than us, be it God, reason, karma, etc, and the development of mindfulness reminiscent of Stoic spiritual exercises which were later taken up into the Christian tradition. Indeed the Christian tradition and the other great religions have produced the figure of the saint, the one who has conquered themselves to become whole and complete. In fact here we strike on a deeper sense of that tricky Greek term, *eudaimonia*, as wholeness or completion, that is, a life that turns out well.

If consumerism threatens us collectively, based as it is on endless growth within a finite world with finite resources, it also threatens the individual in their own lifestyle. A life uncritically given over to consumerism is one of life-long indebtedness, of never ending desire for goods and experiences that very quickly lose their lustre, and a life that is externalised by perpetual distractions, quite apart from the need to work hard in order to eventually pay for all this. We risk becoming lost to ourselves in the unrelieved busyness of modern life.

Consumerism is an idol, a false god that promises so much yet delivers very little of any real worth. Consumerism as an answer to the question what is the good life, must surely fail the test when compared to the reliability and permanence guaranteed by a life governed by intellect, virtue and the quest for wisdom. If 'know thyself!' was the best known divine command inscribed at Delphi, the other one was *mêden agan!*, (nothing in excess!) The discipline of self-knowledge and moderation, I suggest, is itself the consolation of philosophy in a time of recession, but most especially in a time of economic growth.

Further Reading Suggestions:
For a more in-depth treatment of the philosophical critique of the foundations of consumerism see:
Bob Brecher, *Getting what you want? A critique of liberal morality,* Routledge: London, 1998
For an important and accessible study of the therapeutic nature of ancient philosophy see:
Pierre Hadot, *Philosophy as a Way of Life: Spiritual Exercises from Socrates to Foucault,* Wiley-Blackwell: London, 1995

CHAPTER FIVE

The Consolations of Kant's Philosophy

Manfred Welteke

To answer the question what consolation Kant's philosophy has to offer, one will have to turn to his philosophy of religion. This is firmly rooted in his moral philosophy which in turn cannot be understood without a basic introduction to his theory of knowledge. In what follows I will, therefore, after some brief information about Kant's life, give a short introduction first to his theoretical and then to his moral philosophy before finally turning to his philosophy of religion.

I. Kant's life

Immanuel Kant was born in 1724 in Königsberg, the biggest city of what was then East Prussia. Today Königsberg is called Kaliningrad and belongs to the Russian Federation. After Kant finished his studies he first became a private tutor and worked as a librarian until in 1755 he started to lecture in the university. Eventually, in 1770 Kant achieved his life's ambition and became professor of logic and metaphysics in the university of his home town. Kant led a very uneventful life devoted exclusively to his philosophical work. He never left Königsberg or went abroad. In 1797 he stopped lecturing, yet he continued – although unsuccessfully – to work on philosophical problems. He died in 1804.

Kant's philosophy can be characterised as an attempt to find a synthesis between the rival philosophical traditions of rationalism and empiricism. Typically, rationalists believe that it is possible to gain insight and knowledge apart from sense perception and experience. For example, in Plato's dialogue *Meno* Socrates establishes geometrical truths simply by talking to an uneducated slave boy. For empiricists, on the other hand, this describes an impossibility. Locke, for example, claimed that there can be nothing in the understanding which has not previously been in the senses.

While he agreed with rationalists that not all knowledge derives from experience, Kant denied that what we know independently of experience can serve for more than to make experience possible. Initially and before he broke with it, Kant was a philosopher in the rationalist tradition. In his so-called pre-critical period he published a number of different treatises on a variety of topics. Yet from 1770 to 1781 Kant fell silent. In this decade he worked on his *magnum opus*, the *Critique of Pure Reason*, which can without exaggeration be described as one of the most influential philosophical books ever to have been written. Towards the end of the *Critique of Pure Reason* Kant asks three questions which he claimed comprise the whole of philosophy. These are: 1. What can I know? 2. What should I do? 3. What may I hope? (B 833) Let us look at these three questions in turn.

II. What can I know?

What is characteristic of Kant's theoretical philosophy can best be explained by the way he responded to the empiricism of David Hume whom he credited with having woken him from his 'dogmatic slumbers'. However, let us first clarify a few other things. Few sciences are content to merely collect data or to just describe objects. Science looks for explanations. In the natural sciences, to explain something generally means to find the causes of observed phenomena. Thus we might ask: 'Why did that piece of metal expand?' A physicist might tell us that this increase in volume can be explained by the fact that the metal was heated. The work of scientists – at least in the natural sciences – consists to a large extent in the search for such causal relationships.

The Scottish empiricist philosopher David Hume had subjected the concept of causality to a thorough analysis and found that causality is not something we can directly experience. As an empiricist he was therefore consistent when he contended that the concept of causality could not be legitimised by empiricist argument. For empiricists, only what can be traced back to sense impressions has theoretical warrant. This, however, had the consequence that one of the central concepts of science stood on very shaky foundations indeed. According to Hume, the most that can be said is that the concept of cause is based on a customary belief. In his *Treatise of Human Nature* his discussion of the idea of a necessary causal connection culminates in the conclusion that the relationship between cause and effect

> can never operate upon the mind, but by means of custom, which determines the imagination to make a transition from the idea of the one object to that of its usual attendant ... (*Treatise*, p 170)

Kant did not accept this result. He agreed with Hume: the concept of a cause, or the *category* of causality, as – following Aristotle – he called these concepts, cannot be legitimised by an appeal to sense experience. Instead, he provided a different justification of this concept which at the same time explained why concepts of this kind cannot be legitimised by an appeal to experience. Categories cannot be legitimised in this way because, according to Kant, they first make experience possible: categories are conditions for the possibility of experience. An incredible amount of scholarly effort has gone into trying to elucidate how exactly this theory should be understood and its correct interpretation is the subject of an ongoing debate. In my own view, regarding the category of causality, what Kant tried to show is the following: the mere idea of an objective temporal sequence already implies the concept of necessity. So there is a sense in which Hume's doubt comes too late. In order to formulate his doubt about the idea of a necessary connection in time he makes use of the idea of an objective sequence in time. Hume, according to Kant, did not realise that this idea of an objective time sequence already depends on the concept of necessity, because an objective sequence in time implies that my perceptions are necessitated and beyond my control.

Now, if this Kantian argument is sound then we do not need to rely on mere customary belief as the foundation for our use of the crucial concept of causality. Belief would then have been replaced by a philosophical justification and defence of this indispensible concept. Yet Kant claimed also that while the category of causality is an *a priori* concept, i.e. that its origin cannot be traced back to experience alone, it nevertheless cannot be applied outside of experience to get beyond its limits. So although for Kant, like for the rationalists, the concept of cause had its origin in the understanding, he denied that it had any application beyond the limits of experience.

As well as *a priori* forms of thought Kant thought that we also possess two *a priori* forms of intuition: space and time. According to Kant's theory, space and time were neither systems of relations of the things in them (which had been Leibniz's view) nor do they exist independently of them (which Newton thought). Instead, according to Kant, space and time, as forms of intuition, belong to the constitution of finite intellects and thus to the way finite intellects experience a world of objects and events. Clearly, a lot more would need to be said about this, yet there is no space here for a discussion of this controversial doctrine.

After Kant had analysed the human cognitive capacity and its limits in the first half of the *Critique of Pure Reason*, he examined traditional metaphysical knowledge claims and subjected them to a devastating criticism. It is beyond the scope of this chapter to go into any of the fascinating arguments in this part of the First Critique in detail. I will have to briefly summarise Kant's result: he concludes that all the traditional rationalist arguments concerning the human soul and its immortality, the existence and nature of God and of the world as a whole, i.e. concerning its beginning in time and its ultimate constitution, are invalid and worthless. It was Kant's result that any proof of the non-existence of God or of the mortality of the soul transgressed the limits of our knowledge as much as the proof of the opposite. He denied speculative reason all pretensions to insight into transcendent matters and famously claimed that he 'found it necessary to deny knowledge, in order to make room for faith.' (B XXX) Kant thought it was ultimately a good thing that we cannot claim any knowledge regarding the transcendent metaphysical questions, for if such knowledge were our motive for moral action, we would act for fear of punishment or hope of reward and not out of respect for the moral law. Towards the end of his second critique, the *Critique of Practical Reason*, he concludes 'that the unsearchable wisdom by which we exist is not less worthy of admiration in what it has denied than in what it has granted us.' (A 264)

As we will see in the last section, Kant believed that pure

practical reason is entitled to postulate something which in the field of theoretical speculation it has no right to assume (see B 804). However, we should note that although Kant had denied that the design argument, i.e. the proof of God's existence that relies on the order of the world, is valid, (he agreed with Hume that this argument lacks the apodictic certainty required of a proof) he nevertheless thought that this proof deserved our respect (B 651). He thought that the ever-increasing evidence for the systematic order of the world, although merely empirical, was so powerful, that just 'one glance at the wonders of nature and the majesty of the universe' (ibid) could dispel doubts regarding the existence of a supreme author of the world, and even make this conviction 'irresistible'. We will see that this teleological way of looking at the world is characteristic of Kant.

Before we move on to Kant's moral philosophy we need to say one more important thing about his theory of knowledge. Kant thought that the fact that we are in possession of *a priori* knowledge, like the principle of causality briefly looked at earlier, proves that we do not know the world as it is in itself but merely as it appears to us. This is a vexed and much discussed aspect of Kant's theoretical philosophy and subject to an ongoing debate. It is a difficult topic but one we cannot avoid entirely and therefore have to address, however briefly. How can this claim be understood? More argument would be required to support this but I think one can say that the world as we come to know it is experienced relative to a standpoint. I agree with Gardner who maintains that our standpoint is compared by Kant to an absolute standpoint and what characterises our epistemic situation for Kant is the fact that we can make sense of our perspective on reality 'only by referring to a point of view outside it, of which we can form a conception, but which we cannot occupy.'[1] Given this epistemic situation of ours we can never dogmatically claim that everything knowable is all there is, i.e. that it comprises the whole of reality.[2] This must suffice as an exposition of Kant's

1. Gardner, p 303. Chapter 8 of Gardner's guidebook to the First Critique is an excellent introduction to this difficult topic and and offers a most lucid exposition of it.
2. cf Höffe 1983, p 201

answer to the first question: what can I know? Let us now proceed to our second question: What should I do?

II. What should I do?

Central to Kant's moral philosophy is the concept of duty. Kant's moral philosophy appeals strongly to the conscience of individual moral agents. Morality for Kant is not the conformity to the standards of behaviour of a certain group or age. Kant makes a basic distinction between outward behaviour and the motive of such behaviour. Behaviour that conforms to a moral norm is not automatically moral because of that. Rather, what counts is the motive of the behaviour. The opening claim of Kant's *Groundwork of the Metaphysics of Morals* is the following:

> It is impossible to conceive anything at all in the world, or even outside it, which can be taken as good without qualification, except a good will.

What may seem good besides a good will, for example wit, courage and determination, is not good in itself, because it can be bad or hurtful if used by a bad will. The same is true for the blessings of fortune: power, wealth, honour, even health, and the various elements which people take to constitute what they call 'happiness'. Kant thinks that such things can lead to arrogance, vanity and a sense of self-importance. In order to retain their goodness such things must be subjected to a good will. The value of a good will is so overriding that Kant claims that we could not share the joy of a rich person which lacked all signs of a good character. Thus, there seems to be in our basic moral constitution the idea that only a morally good person deserves to be happy. Kant believed that a sober assessment of the human condition should lead one to the view that not happiness but something else is the far higher and nobler purpose of human existence: the *worthiness* of being happy.

Kant's second claim in the *Groundwork* is that a good will is held to be good not by the effects which it produces or by its fitness for a given purpose, by its mere good volition, i.e. it is good in itself. (cf 394) What this means is that morality requires more than just conformity to a set of rules. Only behaviour that is motivated by a respect for the moral law can be called moral. Kant illustrates this with the example of an honest grocer. It is consistent with moral, dutiful conduct for a grocer not to overcharge an inexperienced customer so that, as Kant says, even the ignorance of a child is not going to be exploited. Yet the conduct of such a grocer does not justify our judgement that he has acted honestly out of respect for the moral law: for it was also in his own best interest to behave honestly for otherwise he would get a bad reputation and lose his customers. Kant gives an number of additional examples of which I want us to look at one more because I think that it is often misunderstood. According to Kant we are morally obliged to help others if it is in our power to do so. Yet there are also some people who are of such a benevolent nature, that they enjoy to increase the joy of others simply because of the delight they feel in the satisfaction of seeing the results of their kindness. Kant thinks that in such a case the action, however amiable it is, and also outwardly coinciding with our moral obligations, has no genuine moral worth. We are entitled to praise and highly encourage such behaviour, yet it does not call for moral admiration because the motive was not a purely moral one.

This last example can be and has been read in the following way: It seems to suggest that someone helping reluctantly is morally better than someone who helps gladly and from spontaneous good will. This seems most counter-intuitive and also an unattractive consequence of a moral theory. However, Christine Korsgaard,[3] an influential contemporary Kantian moral philosopher teaching at Harvard, thinks that such an interpretation amounts to a misreading of the example. She ask us to consider the following. Kant makes it clear that his reason for contrasting cases of natural affection with those where the motive of duty works without natural affection is this: the operation of the motive of duty is especially obvious in the later kind of case. Now, this strategy is open to misunderstandings, however, the essential difference between the two people contrasted in the examples does not concern the question whether the helping action is en-

3. See Korsgaard, p 58f

joyed or not. It concerns the question whether one helps only because of the enjoyment or because it is perceived that help is something which it is necessary to give. Nothing prevents any action
from being done from the motive of duty where sympathy is also
present. The person who acts from duty is usually imagined as
someone who does not really care for the happiness of others. Yet
this is simply not true. Duty is not a different purpose, it is a different ground for the adoption of a purpose. Thus Kant's idea is expressed better by saying that the sympathetic person's motive is
shallower than the motive of the morally worthy person. They both
want to help, but to the merely sympathetic person a further stretch
of motivating thought about helping is not available which is available to the person acting from duty first and foremost.

It is time to turn to two questions: What is the moral law and
how does Kant justify it? When Kant talks about the moral law he
does not refer to a historically given moral code. Rather, Kant tries
to determine the content of the moral law. He approaches the sol-
ution to this problem in two steps. He first observes that humans
act according to rules. According to Kant, although everything in
nature occurs according to laws, we humans alone are able to behave according to the representation of a law or rule. Let us look at
some concrete, even trivial example of this. Somebody might say:
'I will not join you at the cinema tonight', replying when asked for
the reason: 'I have been out two nights already this week and that
is my limit.' Now, of course not all human behaviour is principled
in this way and it is another common misrepresentation of Kant's
moral philosophy that he is regarded as a rigourist advising us to
subject every aspect of our lives to moral rules. This is not the case:
he acknowledged that there are plenty of situations when our
choices are morally neutral. But I think he is right to observe that a
lot of what we do follows subjective rules which he called 'maxims' and also that the maxims of human behaviour are countless,
varying as they do with time and circumstance.

Kant's second step is to ask: how do we find the content of the
moral law which will let us select the morally valid maxims of
those of the countless maxims humans may adopt and follow?
Which criterion can we apply to isolate those maxims which qualify

as moral rather than purely subjective and arbitrary rules? We have seen by now that for Kant the moral worth of an action does not depend on realising a particular goal, but on the goodness of the motivating will. The end intended by a given action cannot bestow absolute moral value on it. Given that this is so: in what can this value consist, if it cannot be placed in the relation of the will to the effects of the action? It can only consist in the relation between the will and the principle or maxim according to which the volition came about. This principle of willing is Kant's famous 'categorical imperative'. Kant has provided several formulations for it. Here is the first formula: 'Never act except in such a way that you can also will that your maxim should become a universal law.' (402) We can see from the inclusion of the word 'also' that it would be misleading to interpret Kant's moral philosophy as though it was committed to a view according to which morality is basically an exercise of what one might call 'the mortification of the flesh'. The categorical imperative does not command us to ig- nore our natural impulses, as if all natural desires would have to be expelled from the principles of our actions and replaced by rea- son alone. The categorical imperative merely says that we should be able 'to also will' that the principles of our actions could be uni- versalised. All the categorical imperative obliges us to do is to give reason a decisive influence on the way we lead our lives. An alter- native formula of the categorical imperative is the following:

> ... [M]an and generally any rational being exists as an end in himself, not merely as a means to be arbitrarily used by this or that will, but in all his actions, whether they concern himself or other rational beings, must be always regarded at the same time as an end. (428)

I leave it to your imagination to envisage how different our world would be if this moral law was actually followed. All the most depressing features of our age, the trafficking of women for the sex industry, the routine torture of prisoners, immigrant smug- gling, and the exploitation of workers in its many forms would dis- appear overnight. This must suffice as an introduction to the basic ideas of Kant's moral philosophy. We now turn to our last question.

III. What may I hope?

We saw in the first part of this chapter that it had been one of the results of Kant's *Critique of Pure Reason* that in all questions transcending the limits of experience we cannot attain knowledge. Regarding the philosophy of religion the question Kant asked himself was whether it was possible to justify a form of rational faith. In the area of theoretical reason this was found to be impossible, yet this left the question open whether there were moral arguments that could be advanced in this regard. We saw earlier that for Kant morality could not be reduced to conformity to a set of rules but that it consisted in the conformity of the will of a rational agent to the moral law and that the motive for achieving such conformity was respect for the moral law. Kant thought that it was the life-long moral task of every human being to try to approximate to such conformity. In this context Kant sometimes also talks about the 'sanctification of the will',[4] i.e. the effort to approximate one's volition and choices to ever greater agreement with the moral law. For him it was the degree to which a person had achieved this sanctification, the ultimate and unconditional task of human life, that determined their moral worth. This last claim is the central assumption on which Kant's philosophy of religion is built. Before I say some more about Kant's views in this area of philosophy I want to quote in full a famous passage from the end of the *Critique of Practical Reason* which will help to set the tone for the last section of this chapter:

> Two things fill the mind with ever new and increasing admiration and awe, the more often and the more steadily we reflect on them: the starry heavens above and the moral law within us. I have not to search for them and conjecture them as though they were veiled in darkness or were in the transcendent region beyond my horizon; I see them before me and connect them directly with the consciousness of my existence. The

---

4. See the *Critique of Practical Reason*, A 58: 'This holiness of will is, however, a practical idea, which must necessarily serve as a type to which finite rational beings can only approximate indefinitely, and which the pure moral law, which is itself on this account called holy, constantly and rightly holds before their eyes.'

former begins from the place I occupy in the external world of sense, and enlarges my connection therein to an unbounded extent with worlds upon worlds and systems of systems, and moreover into limitless times of their periodic motion, its beginning and continuance. The second begins from my invisible self, my personality, and exhibits me in a world which has true infinity, but which is traceable only by the understanding, and with which I discern that I am not in a merely contingent but in a universal and necessary connection, as I am also thereby with all those visible worlds. The former view of a countless multitude of worlds annihilates as it were my importance as an animal creature, which after it has been for a short time provided with vital power, one knows not how, must again give back the matter of which it was formed to the planet it inhabits (a mere speck in the universe). The second, on the contrary, infinitely elevates my worth as an intelligence by my personality, in which the moral law reveals to me a life independent of animality and even of the whole sensible world, at least so far as may be inferred from the destination assigned to my existence by this law, a destination not restricted to conditions and limits of this life, but reaching into the infinite. (A 289)[5]

As we see from the final lines of this text, Kant thought that the sanctification of the will is a task that allows of no conclusion in this life: no human agent can reach this goal in his or her lifetime.[6] Kant presents the following argument: it would go against the dignity of the moral law if it is the ultimate moral task of human beings to achieve ever greater conformity to it but if it is also the case that this task simply ends in death. This would seem to undermine the dignity of the moral law, because it would then absurdly command one to pursue a goal that is unreachable. It would also seem to undermine the dignity of the moral agent, because a life-long moral development would simply come to nothing. This is why Kant thought that the immortality of the soul was a 'postulate of pure practical reason'. Practical reason needs

---

5. Probably inspired by Psalm 19.
6. For the following I am indebted to Hans Wagner, *Moralität und Religion bei Kant*, in Wagner 1980, p 345ff

to postulate that the moral progress can continue infinitely and thus will not be ended by death (V, 122-124).

The continued sanctification of the will Kant also calls the 'Highest Good' for moral agents. However, the Highest Good is not the complete good. We saw earlier that Kant thought that a moral way of life establishes the worthiness to be happy. Yet in order to remain worthy of happiness, actual happiness often has to be sacrificed. The complete good is the unity of the worthiness to be happy with the actual happiness deserved. Kant thinks that only this is the unqualified Highest Good. Now, one thing is patently obvious: only the first half of the Highest Good is within our power and if this world is all there is then the Highest Good will never be realised. So if the morally necessary idea of the Highest Good is to be retained a power beyond nature has to be postulated which could bring about and guarantee the congruence between the worthiness to be happy and actual happiness. We have to think of this power as a being with understanding and will which is not indifferent to what is morally deserved. Thus, according to Kant, the existence of God has to be postulated for moral reasons. Again pure practical and not theoretical reason postulates something that theoretical reason is powerless to prove or disprove.

It is important that we take note of the fact that for Kant religion is not the basis of morality. Instead, we saw that for Kant it is the other way round. The basic fact of morality, i.e. the moral law, leads to postulates that are also articles of faith of (at least of some forms of) religion. According to Kant the postulate of God's existence is the only way in which we can make intelligible to ourselves how the Highest Good, i.e. the happiness to the degree a moral agent is worthy of it, is possible. Thus, in a moral respect what is and would forever remain a mere hypothesis of theoretical reason becomes more than that: a postulate of pure rational faith because pure practical reason is its source. In no way must moral obligation be based on religious belief. Kant clearly says in the *Groundwork of the Metaphysics of Morals* that moral philosophy 'is allowed no peg either in heaven or on earth from which to suspend her principles' (4:425) Likewise, the hope of future happiness cannot be the motive for moral conduct. Yet notwithstanding these provisos, Kant says that a pure moral faith can ground a hope that could not be grounded without such a faith. The moral law commands unconditionally to sanctify the will and thus to contribute that part of the Highest Good which alone is within our power, irrespective of the prospect whether the worthiness of being happy will ever be completed by actual happiness. Nobody can know whether this will be the case. This much is certain, however: it will not be the case in this life and has not been the case for countless people who lead morally exemplary lives but had to suffer, often to the point of losing their lives, because of their moral commitment.

We can see that Kant saw it as a necessary implication of the moral life that moral agents must postulate that the stage of moral development they have achieved has an intrinsic claim to be preserved. However, why should God respond to this entitlement? Kant's answer to this question seems to have been the following: The moral law is obligating free agents to approximate their volition and moral choices to ever greater agreement with the moral law. Kant says in the *Critique of Judgement* that to bring free agents (which are the only agents that could be subject to moral laws) into existence could be the only possible ultimate motive for a creator: 'Only of man under moral laws can we say, without transgressing the limits of our insight: his being constitutes the final purpose of the world.' (B 422, fn)

So if the moral self-development was the reason why moral beings were brought into existence in the first place, then this seems to ground a justifiable hope to have the stage of their moral development, reached at the end of a life-long effort to ever greater conformity with the moral law, respected and preserved. That this is what Kant actually thought can be seen from a relevant passage from the Transcendental Dialectic of the First Critique. He says in this passage that if we judged according to the analogy with the nature of living things, of which we assume that nothing in their constitution is without purpose but on the contrary exactly suited for their destiny in life, then we would have to regard humans, who are the only beings that could possibly be the final purpose of the order of the world, as the only beings that are exempt from this analogy, because:

> '[m]an's natural endowments – not merely his talents and the impulses to enjoy them, but above all else the moral law within him – go so far beyond all the utility and advantage which he may derive from them in this present life, that he learns thereby to prize the mere consciousness of a righteous will as being, apart from all advantageous consequences, apart even from the shadowy reward of posthumous fame, supreme over all other values; and so feels an inner call to fit himself, by his conduct in this world, and by the sacrifice of many of its advantages, for citizenship in a better world upon which he lays hold in idea. (B 425)

Finally we may ask: is this consoling? However we answer this question, I think we can agree that it is certainly ennobling and this is what I think Kant wanted most: to inspire us to retain the respect for what can yet become of humanity, if it advances morally, and to work towards a better future, despite the setbacks of history. How much he was in awe of the fact that humans are free moral agents, subject to a moral law, and, as a representative of the enlightenment, ultimately how optimistic that humanity can indeed advance morally, can be seen from the following quotation which will end this chapter:

> What is that inside me, which makes that I can sacrifice the most intimate temptations of my drives and all desires, which proceed from my nature, to a law which promises me no advantage in return and which threatens no loss when I transgress it; nay, which I venerate all the more deeply, the sterner it commands and the less it offers in return? This question excites the whole soul by the amazement over the greatness and sublimity of the inner disposition of humanity and at the same time the impenetrability of the mystery, which it enshrouds (because the answer: it is freedom, would be tautological, because it is that which amounts to this mystery). One cannot focus one's attention on it enough and to admire within oneself a might, which will not give way to any might of nature;

and this admiration is the feeling created by ideas, which, if over and above the doctrines of morality delivered in schools and from pulpits the portrayal of this mystery would form a separate and often repeated concern of the instructors, would sink deep into the soul and not fail to make people morally better.'[7]

---

7. 'On a Newly Arisen Superior Tone in Philosophy', AA 8, 402f

Bibliography:
Works by Kant:
1929. *Critique of Pure Reason*, trs Norman Kemp-Smith, London.
1958. *The Groundwork of the Metaphysics of Morals*, trs H. J. Paton, London.
1987. *Critique of Judgement*, trs Werner Pluhar, Indianapolis.
1998. *Critique of Pure Reason*, trs Paul Guyer, Cambridge.

Secondary Literature:
Bennett, J., 1972, *Kant's Dialectic*, London.
Bennett, J., 1973, *Kant's Analytic*, London.
Bird, G., 2006, *The Revolutionary Kant*, Illinois.
Höffe, O., 2003, *Kants Kritik der reinen Vernunft*, Munich.
Hume, D., 1978, *A Treatise of Human Nature*, Oxford, (ed P. H. Nidditch)
Korsgaard, C., 1996, *The Scources of Normativity*, Cambridge.
Paton, H. J., 1970, *Kant's Metaphysics of Experience*, London.
Strawson, P., 1976, *The Bounds of Sense*, London.
Wagner, H., 1980, *Kritische Philosophie*, Würzburg. (ed K. Bärthlein and W. Flach)

Suggestions for further reading:
Works by Kant:
1958. *The Groundwork of the Metaphysics of Morals*, trs H. J. Paton, London.
1997. *Prolegomena to any Future Metaphysics*, trs Gary Hatfield, Cambridge.

Works on Kant:
Gardner, S., 1999, *Kant and the Critique of Pure Reason*, London.
Guyer, P., 2006, *Kant* (Routledge philosophers), Oxford.
Scruton, R., 2001, *Kant*, Oxford.
Ward, A., 2006, *Kant. The Three Critiques*, Cambridge.
Wood, A., 2005, *Kant*, Oxford.

CHAPTER SIX

The Consolation of Pragmatism

Ciaran McGlynn

At the start of his classic book, *Pragmatism*, William James quotes G. K. Chesterton's idea that you can tell a great deal about a person by knowing what their general view of the universe is.[1] To know their worldview is to know their temperament. James goes on to divide these temperaments into two types: the tender-minded (e.g. religious believers, philosophical idealists, and those who tend towards an optimistic view of the world) and the tough-minded (empirically minded scientists who either reject religion or accord it a low status of merely personal preference and whose optimism 'is apt to be decidedly conditional and tremulous').[2] Our temperament, our view of the cosmos, goes a long way towards influencing our choices and actions. While pragmatists can veer towards being either tender or tough-minded, as a philosophy pragmatism tends to be non-deterministic and allows us to construct a worldview that is open and liberating. There are no pre-established facts and we are better off eschewing the notion of eternal truths to which we must accommodate ourselves.

In this paper I want to consider to what extent the philosophy of pragmatism can be a source of consolation in hard times. To do this I shall look at the works of two pragmatists of markedly different temperaments: the more tender-minded William James, one of the founders of pragmatism, and the tougher-minded

---

1. James, W., 1907, *Pragmatism*, in James. W., 1987, *William James: Writings 1902-1910*, New York, The Library of America, p 487. The Chesterton reference comes from G. K. Chesterton, *Heretics*, 1905. Reissued 2009 by Sam Torode Book Arts, Nashville, p 3

2. Optimism is a recurring motif in James's philosophy. For him it entails openness to a transcendent aspect of, and meaning in, the universe, with the further connotation that the future is not set and is open to human creativity.

Richard Rorty, whose radical form of pragmatism has been seen as dangerous relativism. Contrary to what many philosophers might believe, pragmatism can offer a consoling philosophy in that it enables us both to slough off attempts to have us defined in other people's terms and to transform ourselves through self-re-description.

Pragmatists take a historicist view of our beliefs and truths. For them, it was a major development when it was proposed that truth is something that evolves, that it has a past and will have a future. The truths which we hold today were not those of the past and may be seen as incomplete or wholly erroneous tomorrow. For pragmatists, the term 'truth' does not designate some profound permanent insight into reality, rather it is more of an honorific term used to label a belief which we cannot envisage ever being considered false. Those truths we no longer hold – what we might now term 'false beliefs' – are those beliefs which we, either personally or as a society, no longer designate by the honorific term 'true'.[3] Realising the contingent and historical nature of truth, Rorty maintains, 'has helped us substitute Freedom for Truth as the goal of thinking and social progress'.[4] While not all pragmatists would agree that the goal of truth should be replaced with the goal of freedom, a common denominator among pragmatists is the denial of truth as an absolute; the denial of 'Truth' with a capital 'T' (i.e. a 'Truth' that is immune to change in the light of future experience). For pragmatists, truths are made, they are not discovered. A new fact (i.e. an alleged truth) comes along and it must be grafted on to the pre-existing body of truths, in the process a new truth is created. How the previous body of truths is assembled determines what place, if any, a new fact will enjoy in the ever-evolving body of truth. Holders of different bodies of truth will assimilate a new fact differently.[5]

3. For example, prior to the success of the Copernican revolution most people would have said that the sun revolved around the earth; it was not only a 'truth', but an obvious 'truth'. This once strongly held belief is now considered false.
4. Rorty, R., 1989, *Contingency, irony, and solidarity*, Cambridge: CUP
5. The nature of the fact, or if it is to be judged a new fact at all, will depend on the viewpoints of the holders of different bodies of truths.

As pragmatists believe that no view is immune to change – including their own views – they are much less likely to be fanatical about their current beliefs. While pragmatists may consciously choose to devote their lives to some ideal or, even, to sacrifice their lives, temperamentally they are far less likely to be extremists. To be an extremist one has to have unbounded faith in the truth of one's beliefs. But those who are aware of the contingency of their beliefs are unlikely to believe that their worldview must be as compelling for others as it is for themselves. A pragmatist is very unlikely to strap a suicide vest to himself; persuasion, not coercion, is the pragmatists preferred *modus operandi*.

But why should pragmatism seem like an appropriate philosophy for hard times? Why should the apparently shifting and uncertain sands of a pragmatist outlook seem a likely place to find solace in a world where certainty is in short supply? Pragmatism seems unconsoling because it denies the absolute nature of traditionally held truths. Hence it can look like the wrong philosophy in a time of hardship because it seems to kick away many of the props that appear to give our lives meaning during periods of crisis. God, religion, absolute moral values, patriotism, all seem to become just so many contrived notions that have no real standing outside of the minds of those who happen to believe in them.

I want to argue that pragmatism, since its conception, has been a philosophy of hope, in that it offers us a view of ourselves and of the world that is full of possibility, free from the very props that not so much bolster up our worldview as constrain it. By freeing ourselves from absolutes we are free to create the guiding principles that best suit our times. Pragmatism is not a radical free-for-all, but a philosophy that recognises the importance of ethnicity, tradition, and contingency as shaping forces in any emerging worldview. Pragmatists like James and Rorty do not advocate a revolutionary discarding of traditions; rather, they wish us to recognise that these traditions are not absolutes and can be changed.

James's Pragmatism

William James (1842-1910) was not only an outstanding philosopher but was also one of the founders of the discipline of psychology. The brother of the novelist, Henry James, he taught at Harvard for many years. He saw pragmatism as steering between the two major philosophic temperaments that had dominated the western outlook for centuries: the tender-minded rationalists and the tough-minded empiricists. Like the rationalists, James's pragmatism is sympathetic to religion. Like the empiricists, he gives great importance to sensory experiences. But, unlike the empiricists, James's pragmatism 'has no materialistic bias'.[6] Tough-minded empiricists, such as natural scientists, tend to have a materialist metaphysics as their default view of the universe. James, on the other hand, will embrace a wide range of experiences, including mystical ones, so long as they have practical consequences.

This notion of practical consequences is key for James's pragmatism. His pragmatism had two aspects: first, it was a method for solving, or dissolving, intellectual problems. If a dispute did not have practical consequences in terms of experience, then it was vacuous. The second key aspect of pragmatism was its theory of truth. For James: 'Truth lives ... on a credit system. Our thoughts and beliefs "pass", so long as nothing challenges them, just as bank-notes pass so long as nobody refuses them'[7] There is no truth that is not subject to revision in the light of future experience. 'The "absolutely" true ... is that ideal vanishing-point towards which we imagine our temporary truths will some day converge.'[8] What we call true today may be deemed false tomorrow. For James, a truth is something that we can verify; and verification was seeing how well the truth agreed with reality. However, this idea of agreeing with reality did not mean what it did for many positivist philosophers[9] – an empirically testable way of ground-

6. James, W., 1907, *Pragmatism*, in James. W., 1987, *William James: Writings 1902-1910*, New York, The Library of America, p 518
7. Ibid, pp 576-7
8. Ibid, p 583
9. The positivists were those philosophers, starting with the French philosopher Auguste Comte (1798-1857), who sought to replace philosophy, especially metaphysics, by natural science.

ing a belief in sense experience. The reality one's truth had to agree with included, but was not confined to, physical reality available through sense experience. Reality included physical facts, 'abstract kinds of things', and the relation between all of these, but, crucially, reality also included 'the whole body of other truths already in our possession'.[10]

James believed that for a philosophy to be plausible it must cater for the 'feelings' of ordinary people. 'The finally victorious way of looking at things will be the most completely *impressive* way to the normal run of minds.'[11] But the normal run of minds can be a very conservative tribunal and extremely reluctant to incorporate new truths. James pointed out that when we are faced with phenomena so novel that to accept their existence would disturb our network of other beliefs, our usual reaction is simply to ignore the phenomena and, even, 'to abuse those who bear witness for them'.[12]

James saw pragmatism as being essentially a philosophy of hope in that it envisioned a universe still in the making, one in which human creativity played an essential role. While making full use of the naturalistic or scientific approach to understanding the world, it does not fall into the metaphysical assumptions of so many reductionist scientists of seeing the world as ultimately determined and purposeless. Pragmatists, like James, see the benefits of ideas such as those of a benevolent God who has designed the world and of human beings possessing freewill. In the absence of such beliefs, naturalism can lead to a vision of a world in which everything that can happen has been written from the start, and what will ultimately happen is the death of all living beings in the universe. For James, there is no compelling reason,

---

10. James, W., 1907, *Pragmatism*, in James. W., 1987, *William James: Writings 1902-1910*, New York, The Library of America, p 578. While James extends the notion of reality beyond the empirically verifiable, he does seem to cling to the notion that in some remote way all truths will be relatable, in principle at least, to some sense experience. (p 580)

11. Ibid, p 503. As we shall see, Richard Rorty would disagree that there can be a finally victorious way of looking at things.

12. Ibid, p 513. James, who took an active interest in psychic research, was probably speaking from personal experience.

other than personal preference, to accept such a bleak scenario. The religious impulse, on the contrary, is not irrational and with its innate optimism in the existence of a transcendent source of meaning is pragmatically to be welcomed.

For James, we play a creative role in the universe – we add to it: 'The world stands really malleable, waiting to receive its final touches at our hands ... Man *engenders* truths upon it.'[13] Consequently, Jamesian pragmatism is a truly revolutionary philosophy. It is more consoling than philosophies which hold that truth is out there, ready-made. For pragmatists, no situation is the true and unalterable state of affairs – all are capable of being changed, improved, re-made. There are no facts of the matter that we must stoically accept – we create our own world, our own truths, and our own future. As I shall argue in the conclusion, even the so-called facts of common sense are 'facts' because we choose to designate them so. Even in such hard cases as serious illness there is scope for how we choose to interpret the 'facts' and how we choose to define ourselves in the light of these facts.

Rorty's Pragmatism

Richard Rorty (1931-2007) was the most influential pragmatic philosopher of the late twentieth and early twenty-first centuries. Rorty was a precocious youngster who went to university at the age of fifteen. His early career was distinguished but neither brilliant nor contentious. He rose to notoriety in 1979 with the publication of his *Philosophy And The Mirror of Nature*, a work which called into question what had been taken to be the traditional aim of philosophy: the discovery of 'Truth'. Rorty had drifted from the dominant analytic philosophy of the time to the philosophy of pragmatism to which he gave a new turn. In 1989 he wrote another seminal work, *Contingency, Irony, and Solidarity*, in which he emphasised the ethical aspect of his work. Later pragmatism is usually referred to as 'neo-pragmatism', to distinguish it from the early pragmatism of Charles Saunders Peirce, William James, and John Dewey. The trend within neo-pragmatism has been towards radicalism, with Rorty representing the most extreme formulation

---

13. Ibid

yet of the pragmatist position. The common thread running through all stages of pragmatism has been an emphasis on the contingent nature of truth.

A key theme of Rorty's is the contingency of language; we cannot 'step outside the various vocabularies we have employed and find a metavocabulary which somehow takes account of all possible vocabularies'.[14] Different vocabularies correspond to radically different ways of speaking about the world, e.g. an Aristotelian as opposed to a post-Galilean way of describing reality. For Rorty, there is no neutral standpoint from which to judge two competing vocabularies. As the criterion of rationality is taken from one's own vocabulary, each vocabulary will appear rational from within its own boundaries, while opposing vocabularies can appear irrational. To Aristotelians the new science was deficient in its overall grasp of the nature of the world; to the followers of Galileo the Aristotelian worldview was outdated, grossly inefficient at predicting events, and laden with untestable hypotheses.

There is no Archimedean point outside of all vocabularies on which we can stand to judge which vocabulary is the right one; the world does not speak a vocabulary, only we do. 'The fact that Newton's vocabulary lets us predict the world more easily than Aristotle's does not mean that the world speaks Newtonian.'[15] When people found out what they could do with Galileo's and Newton's vocabulary they became uninterested in using Aristotle's.[16] Adopting of new vocabularies is the agent of cultural change. The rediscovery of Aristotle's vocabulary in the Middle Ages, the creation of a mathematical way of describing nature in the sixteenth century, the development of a Freudian vocabulary in the twentieth century are all examples of how 'a talent for speaking differently' can provide people with a vocabulary to change their worldview. When a radically new vocabulary catches on, the users of that vocabulary see the world differently from their predecessors.

14. Rorty, R., 1989, *Contingency, irony, and solidarity*, Cambridge: CUP, p. xvi
15. Ibid, p 6
16. Ibid, p 19

Rorty borrows Wittgenstein's tool metaphor of language.[17] Rather than seeing the words we use as a depiction of reality (a view dominated by ocular metaphors of picturing or mirroring) it is more useful, he argues, to see language as a set of tools that enable us to do things in the world. Just as there are many different tools for manipulating the world, none of which is the only, or 'right' tool, so too there is no one set of words that is the 'true' way of talking about the world. In formulating a vocabulary, or assessing someone else's proposed vocabulary, utility, not truth, should be the goal of our inquiry: 'There are as many different useful tools as there are purposes to be served.'[18]

For Rorty, each of us carries around a set of words which we use to justify our actions and beliefs; these are the words of last resort when we are called upon to give a rationale for the truths we hold and the form of life we live. This he calls our 'final vocabulary' in that if doubt is cast upon it we have no other vocabulary to call on to justify it; no non-circular way of justifying our beliefs.[19] Our final vocabulary consists of words like: 'good', 'right', 'true', 'decency', 'the church', and 'the cause'.

A common criticism of Rortian and earlier pragmatism, is that it is disproved by 'common sense'. We know through common sense, it is claimed, that certain things are true. The physical world, it is said, will rapidly disabuse us if we think certain truths are merely contingent. Rorty's attitude to common sense is that it is 'the watchword of those who unselfconsciously describe everything important in terms of the final vocabulary to which they and those around them are habituated'.[20] There is a difference between saying 'the world is out there' and saying 'truth is out there'. To say that the world is out there is merely to recognise that most things that exist are not the product of human mental states. The world can help to regulate those propositions to which we ascribe the term 'truth', but 'truth' is not out there, for 'where there

17. Wittgenstein, L., 1953, *Philosophical Investigations*, Oxford: Blackwell. Section 23.
18. Rorty, R., 1989, *Contingency, irony, and solidarity*, Cambridge: CUP, p 54
19. Ibid, p 73
20. Ibid, p 74

are no sentences there is no truth'.[21] The world does not divide itself up into 'sentence-shaped chunks called facts'.[22] Pragmatists do not claim that they have discovered 'the truth' that there is no truth; they merely claim that we would be better off if we no longer sought a chimera called the 'Truth', and settled for finding truths that served our contingent and ever-changing purposes. Critics of Rorty may argue that he is denying the existence of the 'objective world'. Rorty is not denying that there is a world; what he is calling into question is what his critics mean by 'objective'. If 'objective' means the way things are, irrespective of any observer or description, then he would say that this is the same old chimera being sought – the search for Truth with a capital 'T'. For Rorty, we are better off not chasing will-of-the-wisps such as absolute objectivity or absolute truth.

Rorty believes that the ideal denizen of his liberal society would be a thoroughly pragmatic figure called the 'liberal ironist'. Such citizens would be liberal in that they would hold 'that cruelty is the worst thing we do'. They are ironists in that they also hold that there is no non-circular way open to them to defend their basic liberal credo and are fully aware that their final vocabulary is a wholly contingent affair. If they had lived in a different time or place, or had been reared differently, they could conceivably hold a different set of beliefs. While the ironist cannot claim that his vocabulary is a better match with reality than any other, he is constantly on the lookout for ways of improving his worldview to enable him to achieve the primary goal of his liberal society – the goal of increasing solidarity amongst people. Rorty thinks that solidarity should replace the quest for truth and objectivity. The ideal of solidarity requires us to recognise that one thing human beings have in common is their ability to suffer. Not only can humans experience physical pain, but they can also undergo humiliation, a type of suffering unique to humans. Again, there is no non-circular way that a liberal can argue for the propositions that we should seek solidarity with others and try to alleviate their suffering. Such a sense of solidarity is unlikely to be brought about by

21. Ibid, p 5
22. Ibid

philosophical treatises; the agents of social change are more likely to be artists and journalists. The novel, the TV docudrama, and the movie can do more than any philosopher in forwarding the cause of human solidarity. Rorty points out that Dickens's novels did more to bring about social change than the collected works of all the British social theorists of his day. Likewise, Orwell's *Nineteen Eighty-Four* alerted many westerners to the evils of Soviet society long before philosophers got around to criticising the regime.

The ironist cannot claim to give the 'right description', he can only speak of a 'better description', but only from the standpoint of his final vocabulary. All the ironist can do is tell his story and through it hope to convert his opponent into adopting a liberal vocabulary. There is no neutral point on which he and his opponent can stand; each speaks from within his own final vocabulary. So long as free discussion can take place, Rorty believes, the liberal society can be achieved. One of his famous catchphrases is: 'Take care of freedom and truth will take care of itself.' We should be content, he believes, to call 'true' or 'good' whatever emerges from such free discussion. The essential thing is that we maintain a society in which uncoerced agreement can be achieved.

Two Pragmatisms?

It is not at all certain that William James would have felt comfortable with Richard Rorty's interpretation of pragmatism. In the same way as the inventor of pragmatism, C. S. Peirce, thought that James's version of his theory was not what he understood by pragmatism, so too James would recognise Rorty's neo-pragmatism as an evolutionary development of his views, but would have not endorsed Rorty's wholesale opposition to metaphysics. For James, pragmatism is primarily a method for solving metaphysical disputes,[23] whereas Rorty sees no use for metaphysics and believes that metaphysical disputes can, at best, be dissolved, not solved.

It is on the topics of God and religion that we see a marked difference between the temperaments of James and Rorty. For James, religious belief can be legitimate if one's prior tradition

23. James, op. cit., p 506

and experiences have included elements of a religious outlook. He maintained that personal experience plays a significant role in disposing one to believe in God. Rorty, on the other hand, does not seem to attach much significance to personal experience (e.g. highly subjective mystical experience) in the forming of one's beliefs. He sees any belief in God as a quest after absolute truths and maintains that we would be better off not seeking such absolutes. This difference in temperaments between the two philosophers results in different degrees of optimism in their philosophies. While James's brand of pragmatism is optimistic on both the day-to-day affairs of human beings and in terms of their cosmic outlook, Rorty's pragmatism lacks cosmic optimism. For Rorty, we have it within our power to make things anew, to construct human institutions that will lessen suffering and promote human freedom. Unlike James, he does not see grounds for cosmic optimism and views the religious impulse as something deleterious in the history of human affairs. In its postulation of absolute truth, religion, for Rorty, stymies the free creation of newer and better narratives.

A similarity between James and Rorty is that they see theories as instruments that allow us to do things. If a theory did not have some pragmatic benefit it would soon face extinction. The main similarity between the two philosophers is that they both give up the notion of 'Truth' with a capital 'T'. However, for James, this eschewing of the search for absolute truth is done on the basis that such overarching truths are probably unattainable. James does not rule out, in principle, the existence of such truths; there may be a God. What James is opposed to is the setting up of 'absolute truths' based on evidence and arguments that could always be interpreted differently. As we have seen, an absolute truth for James is a truth with a capital 'T', i.e. a truth that is immune to change in the light of future experience. But experience, for James, is not just sensing, there is also subjective experience which may point to the existence of God or some other type of transcendent reality. Furthermore, James is not averse to the idea that our truths could, in an ultimate sense, line up with our experiences; that there could be a final truth. But, if there is such a thing as a final truth, its finality will rest on nothing more secure than what society has come to agree on.

Rorty, on the other hand, is hostile to any notion of an ultimate truth or to any other absolute that claims to represent anything external to human minds.[24] There is no independent reality or principle we can appeal to to validate any of our narratives. This is how he differs most strikingly from James; he will not allow for the possibility of a permanent transcendent source of truth external to human theorising. A reason for this difference is that Rorty does not give weight to subjective human experience. For Rorty, all is narrative – the narrative is occasionally buffeted by something called the external world, but it is not something that depicts this world or matches its contours. We do not know if reality has contours and there is no way of stepping outside of our narratives to see if any of them accurately maps the contours of the world. Other than through past narratives and current sensory experiences there is no way that we can fabricate new narratives that will help us get on better with the world. Although new narratives may help us do things we could not do before (cure diseases, find new sources of energy, etc) none of these narratives will be 'true' in an absolute sense.

Rorty's Radicalism
Even to fellow pragmatists Rorty seems to have gone too far. There is a lingering notion among many of his detractors that all

---

24. Those examples of absolute truths which are often cited are usually anodyne truths, so trivial that no one will get excited over them one way or the other. (It is probably the fact that they are not ordinarily challenged that gives them the appearance of eternal truths.) Examples such as 'there is now a mug of coffee in front of me' or 'Ciarán believes that there is a mug of coffee in front of him' are usually given as the type of 'truth' that no further experience will ever alter. First of all, it is not obvious that such beliefs are immune to alteration – our inability to imagine how some beliefs could be doubted is no guarantee that they will not be altered under some extraordinary circumstances. Secondly, it is extremely difficult to get from beliefs/'truths' such as those to the philosophically interesting 'truths' about the nature of the world, the existence of God, or the immortality of the soul.

beliefs about the world are not merely formulations of words and, hence, cannot be reduced to being just one more element in a narrative; and that there are features of reality which we know, in a strong sense, and which are immune to revision in the light of any future experience. But, Rorty's critics have found it remarkably difficult to formulate their metaphysical and epistemological certainties in a manner invulnerable to Rortian re-description.

However, Rorty's philosophy is open to objections on the more traditional pragmatic grounds that it will not work. For Rorty, we should replace talk about truth and the quest for truth with the quest for freedom and solidarity. But freedom and solidarity as important moral issues only arose to their present importance in Western society in the context of a culture that believed in absolute truths. The notion of solidarity among humans came about because of the belief that there was something essential that united all human beings – something that constituted human nature. Socrates, the first Western philosopher to propose that we should do good, not harm, to others, made his proposal on the basis that we all possess a soul and that it was for the benefit of our souls that we should do good to one another. Jesus proposed that we should love our neighbour as ourselves because we were essentially all God's creatures. The idea of individual freedom got its greatest boost from thinkers such as Locke who argued that we should be allowed to pursue our own ideal of absolute truth free from persecution of those who had a different notion of absolute truth.

All these advances towards the ideals that Rorty would enshrine in his liberal society arose in the context of thinkers who believed in absolute truths. Now the fact that the ideals of freedom and solidarity arose in the context of the search for Truth with a capital 'T' does not entail that these notions are in any way dependent on such a notion of absolute truth. However, it does suggest that the ideals of solidarity and freedom are delicate plants that might not survive in environments in which ironists have dispensed with the ideal of absolute truth. For many, the pursuit of freedom and the obligation to show solidarity are absolute truths. Freedom and solidarity, seen merely as cultural preferences which may be dispensed with if the *Zeitgeist* of the culture were to change, does not create the right conditions for these moral precepts to thrive. It might well be that a society that does not have Truth will not long retain freedom and solidarity.

Another demerit of Rorty's position is that he does not adequately take account of personal experience. Pragmatically, if one's life experiences have led to belief in God then this is an absolute – one which should not fall out of your final vocabulary. In fact, your personal conviction should compel you to believe that God should be part of everyone's final vocabulary. This is a weakness of Rorty's neo-pragmatism: it is too much of a rationalist philosophy. Beliefs may be held on grounds other than tradition, utility, and rational coherence. One can have private and, maybe, ineffable, experiences that can lead one to have unique insights of 'The Truth'. There need not be compelling reasons for others to subscribe to your 'Truth', but such experiences are compelling for the individual who has had them. Such people cannot become ironists; they have no reason to believe that their vocabulary will change. In all probability, their belief, based on their experiences, is that any future experience will only confirm them in their convictions.

Rorty seems to have a limited conception of what counts as experience. This stems from his restricted view of what it is to be a human being and his conviction that all human experience is narrative. 'For it is essential to my view that we have no pre-linguistic consciousness to which language needs to be adequate, no deep sense of how things are which it is the duty of philosophers to spell out in language'.[25] This limited notion of human experience makes his ironic stance seem more plausible. His idea that everything is text seems to suggest that he does not realise that personal experience can bring a conviction that might enable one either to 'know' that a particular narrative is the right account or feel that one has grasped a truth that cannot be adequately expressed in any narrative.

---

25. Rorty, op. cit., p 21

Conclusion

Rorty's pragmatism can seem a little unconsoling in that it counsels us to reject any notion of absolute truths. However, this abandoning of absolutes has more impact on metaphysical hopes than on practical everyday affairs. Just as Westerners are unconcerned with the metaphysical implications of their science, in time they would probably be equally blasé about the loss of spurious metaphysical absolutes stemming from the adoption of a new philosophy. Nevertheless, given the metaphysical predilections of many of us, Rorty's pragmatism can seem a little extreme. Being extreme does not make his philosophy unconsoling, it just makes it unpalatable. The philosophy that is likely to be the most consoling in troubled times would be a hybrid of James's and Rorty's pragmatism. James personalises the truth, but sees no problem with people coherently maintaining overarching cosmic beliefs, such as belief in God. For James we do not have to be ironical about our beliefs – some of our truths, even if not designated with a capital 'T', are likely to stand the test of time. We do not have to embrace, as Rorty does, the inevitable supersedence of our treasured beliefs. As most people feel the need for such overarching truths James's philosophy seems a more consoling prospect. The aspect of Rorty's philosophy that could be included in the hybrid form of pragmatism is the notion that we can always re-describe our condition and cease to have ourselves defined by the views and categories of others. In this power of re-description Rorty's pragmatism allows us to see that there is no confining reality that condemns us to play particular roles.

Such a hybrid pragmatism would be optimistic on three levels. First, it offers what I would call 'cosmic hope' – the world is open to further creation; it is not necessarily determined by unalterable 'facts'. Secondly, such a pragmatism would endorse social hope. Pragmatists emphasise that we can and in many parts of the world have made life better. No social system is set in stone, all can be changed and improved in furtherance of the general aim of reducing human suffering. Thirdly, pragmatism offers personal hope – we can change ourselves through re-description. This is the main contribution from Rortian pragmatism: it offers the individual a liberating and optimistic outlook. We are not constrained by some abstract and immovable state of affairs called 'the facts' or 'the way things are'. What constitutes the facts of our life that will guide or constrain our future actions are largely up to us. The most limiting constraints are the restrictions we set on our own thinking and creativity. Pragmatism inspires an open view of the future; there is much scope for personal choice, especially if we can free ourselves from any type of fatalistic worldviews.

The nay-sayers, predictably, appeal to the so-called 'facts' of science and common sense to insist that there is a way things are and that this is the deciding factor in our freedom to act. However, it is notoriously difficult to get from scientific and common sense facts to either abstract theories about the world which are absolutely 'true', or to guidance on what should be done. The reason is that 'facts' do not interpret themselves or point to a single course of action. Other background factors come into play: beliefs, experiences, and aspirations. No set of facts is susceptible to just one interpretation; any interpretation or any course of action is underdetermined by the available evidence. Just as facts by themselves do not determine large scale theories so too, on the smaller scale of individual human lives, no set of facts defines the person and forces only one self-conception or one course of action. We do not have to be subjected to descriptions imposed on us by others. No one description of you is the one, the only, the right, description. We are not only free, but compelled, to continually re-describe ourselves. If we choose to adopt the same old descriptions – the ones that others have devised – then we have chosen to become a mere object, an item in someone else's narrative. The liberating thing about pragmatism is that there never is, nor can there be, just one story to tell about ourselves, one way of interpreting the facts of our lives. What we accept as the salient facts depends on what we want to do or achieve. The facts do not choose themselves, nor can they interpret themselves.

We undergo self-transformation throughout our lives. Some periods, for instance the transition from youth to adulthood, are more profound and speedier than other periods. But self-transformations rarely come about as a result of intellectual argument;

they are conversions in which people give up central aspects of their final vocabulary in favour of new ways of speaking both about the world and about themselves. In such conversions people may be as surprised at the transformation as are their friends. We sometimes find that we are speaking a different final vocabulary from the one we did ten or twenty years earlier. There is no particular turning point, no revelatory experience, no devastating argument that can be pointed to as the cause of our transformation; we are surprised to find ourselves voicing sentiments that our younger selves would have baulked at.

Such conversions point to two conclusions. The first is that self-transformation is possible. The second is that such conversions rarely come about as a result of intellectual argument or the systematic application of the principles of common sense. There is usually no compelling reason to change the general worldview aspect of one's final vocabulary; the books one reads and the people one encounters will usually act as the catalyst for such change. However, there may be good reasons to change that part of our final vocabulary which has to do with self-description. If our present self-description is inhibiting, negative, or hopeless, it would be important to change it. The pragmatist's consoling message is that there is nothing, no state of affairs, which is beyond re-description. An interpretative theory, be it of the universe or of one's personal life is a construct, an interpretation of the evidence. If a person's current interpretation is negative, destructive, or confining, it is comforting to know that the interpretation is not written in stone.

Those items of experience that we call 'facts', be they the facts of the universe or the facts of our lives, do not choose themselves. We can always de-emphasise certain facts and emphasise others. The important point is that we can re-describe ourselves and our condition more easily than we can describe the currently accepted facts of the universe. The contemporary theories of how things are on a macro-scale have been constructed by thousands, if not tens of thousands, of individuals over hundreds of years – yet even this edifice is not immune from re-description. The facts of our individual lives do not have this weight of history; their interpretations are much more open and fluid. Rather than looking outside of ourselves for consoling messages from the cosmos, pragmatism teaches us that we are, and always have been, the sole source of consolation. It is humanity, not the cosmos, that is the bearer of glad tidings.

CHAPTER SEVEN

The Consolations of Atheism

Peter Simons

There are two means of refuge from the miseries of life: music and cats.
Albert Schweitzer

A Story

When in 1776 the great Scottish philosopher and critic of religion David Hume lay in his Edinburgh home 'just a-dying', James Boswell travelled to Hume's house to interview him about his attitude to death. Boswell found Hume

> alone, in a reclining posture in his drawing-room. He was lean, ghastly, and quite of an earthy appearance ... He was quite different from the plump figure which he used to present ... He seemed to be placid and even cheerful ... He said he was just approaching to his end ... I had a strong curiosity to be satisfied if he persisted in disbelieving a future state even when he had death before his eyes. I was persuaded from what he said, and from his manner of saying it, that he did persist. I asked him if it was not possible that there might be a future state. He answered it was possible that a piece of coal put upon the fire would not burn; and he added that it was a most unreasonable fancy that we should exist for ever ... I asked him if the thought of annihilation never gave him any uneasiness. He said not the least; no more than the thought that he had not been, as Lucretius observes. ... He said he had no pain, but was wasting away. I left him with impressions which disturbed me for some time.[1]

Neither Boswell nor Samuel Johnson could take seriously Hume's equanimity in the face of his own annihilation and

---

1. *The Journals of James Boswell, 1760-1795*, selected and edited by John Wain, London: Heinemann, 1990, 247-250

thought him to be mad or lying. Incredulous crowds gathered outside Hume's house to see whether he would recant at the last. He never did. But I take Hume at his word, because I have seen a similar case before. My own agnostic father, who believed in no afterlife, faced death by cruel and painful cancer, after only two years of a keenly anticipated retirement, with a peaceful resignation which according to his friend, the local vicar, he had never seen in a religious person. Others no doubt, in the words of Dylan Thomas, 'Rage, rage against the dying of the light.' Each of us will find out in turn how we will react to our own impending demise. But the cases of Hume and my father indicate that unbelievers can face the end calmly and without despair.

The Possible Health Benefits of Religious Belief

It may seem odd, bizarre, even perverse to think that atheism may provide us with consolation in this life. After all, one of the principal benefits of holding a religious belief is widely considered to be the consolatory value of so doing. In the face of death, pain, suffering, evil, wickedness, tragedy, folly, injustice, and all the other unpleasantnesses of life, great and small, to believe in the fundamental goodness of the universe as guaranteed by a divine agency is comforting and is known to afford psychological fortitude to those who are in difficult situations. On that account I might as well wrap up this paper now and go out and hope or pray for salvation, or trudge on miserably waiting for the final curtain, or have a stiff drink, or administer some other sensitivity-reducing chemical substance.

On the other hand, it is an interesting question whether those who, for whatever reason and by whatever path, have come to sincerely deny the existence of a deity are as a matter of statistics typically more miserable, more downcast, more suicidal, more pessimistic, or more cynical than believers. Many believers are quite sure they must be less happy because they have no religious belief to buoy them up in hard times. But that question is not one that can be answered by armchair speculation or by hunch or by asking a few friends. It is one for a proper social survey, using established sociological and statistical methods. Because the issue is one about which people tend to get quite agitated, it is not easy to find an unbiased survey. There are some statistical indications that religious believers are less likely to commit suicide, not because they are less likely to be depressed, but because their belief system makes suicide a wrong action and they are thereby motivated to resist suicidal leanings. It is also the case that religious communities can often offer a ready-made circle of caring and sympathetic people ready and willing to help those of their number who are in a bad state. These are, however, not the benefits of belief, but the benefits of belonging. On the other hand, a survey led by the German clinical psychologist Franz Buggle claims that, contrary to popular opinion, atheists are no more prone to depression than religious people, and indeed less prone than religious people who do not abide by the tenets of their religion and suffer from a bad conscience.[2] So it's not clear what and whom to believe.

I suggest therefore that we leave these questions about the psychological benefits of belief on one side, for two reasons. Firstly, whatever the truth of that matter, it is obviously extremely hard rationally to talk yourself into a belief simply for the sake of your health, where you have other good reasons to disbelieve. And secondly, for those who already are atheists, the question is not whether they would have been better or worse off as believers, but to what extent their lack of belief, or better, their disbelief, does or can afford them any kind of consolation.

Negative Consolations

I shall argue that atheists, whose worldview is characterised in this respect at least by a negative belief, a belief that there is no God, are freed by that negative belief from a number of the burdens that believers have to bear. These burdens are connected with what one might call the three 'S's: sin, sex, and salvation. I don't claim that these are all the things of which unbelievers are disemburdened: for example they are also absolved of the re-

2. Franz Buggle, Dorothee Bister, Gisela Nohe, Wolfgang Schneider and Karl Uhmann, 'Are atheists more depressed than religious people?' *Free Inquiry* 20, 4 (2000). Accessed at http://www. secular humanism. org/library/fi/buggle_20_4.html

quirement regularly to attend church, mosque, synagogue or temple, freeing up time they can devote to other activities. Between the ages of five and fifteen I spent something like a thousand hours of my life attending church, or to put it another way, forty days and forty nights. Could I have done something better with that time? At that age, probably not. Despite its failing to achieve its religious aim, that time was not wasted, since it implanted within me an admiration for the beautiful language of the Anglican liturgy, a love of singing that I still exercise, and a passion for ecclesiastical architecture that still drives me to cathedrals before any other building in a city I visit for the first time. But I am now delighted to spend Sunday mornings doing other things.

Being absolved of religiously based guilt, remorse and other negative attitudes and emotions about sin, sex and salvation are powerful reasons why an atheist may be grateful not to bear believers' burdens.

Let's start with sin. I'll introduce it again with a personal anecdote. The last time I attended a church service as distinct from visiting a church for touristic, family or cultural reasons was on 17 February 2008. The attendance was somewhat involuntary. I was participating in a conference in the Dutch city of Delft, made pictorially famous by the great Jan Vermeer, and wandering across the main square early on the Sunday evening before the conference started I heard singing coming from the main church on the square, the Nieuwe Kerk (New Church), a marvellous brick Gothic building. The singing was reminiscent of Anglican choral evensong, so I put my head round the door thinking to listen for a few minutes. I was at once taken by the hand by a man dressed in black and whisked peremptorily across the church to a seat prominently visible, and given a hymn book and a pair of earphones. The hymns and psalms were simple Protestant fare, easy to sight-read, but after five minutes of this the singing ceased and the preacher mounted a high pulpit laterally across the nave to address the sideways-facing congregation, all of whom were strictly dressed in black and white, the women with black hats, the men with black suits, white shirts and black ties, the children also monochrome. My passive Dutch is too poor to have caught more than part of the preacher's message, but the earphones allowed me a full simultaneous translation into English, by a hidden interpreter stationed there purely for the scarce likes of myself. My seat being in full view of the congregation, I could not in politeness leave for the three quarters of an hour that the sermon lasted: held there a social prisoner I was forced to listen to the most appalling sermon I have ever heard. The preacher was intent on impressing everyone with the importance of death, how modern tendencies paid it too little attention, how the young should be confronted with it as soon as possible, and how the only way to be assured of survival was to be one of the elect, predestined for salvation by God, independently of one's actions. Everyone, unbelievers, Jews, Moslems, apostates, Romans, and even Martin Luther, had a false understanding, all that is except for John Calvin and his followers. All of this was delivered in a calm, reasonable-sounding mellifluous Dutch voice bereft of the haranguing tone of evangelistic and charismatic preachers from elsewhere in the Protestant spectrum. The congregation looked suitably dour and worried throughout. As soon as the music started again I quickly left, in relief but also in a quiet rage at the miserable, grinding, inhuman, joyless, in a word, puritan religion of the Dutch Reformed Church. I swore never again to attend one of their services. My hosts later told me that Delft was in the middle of the Dutch Bible Belt, and what I had witnessed was standard fare.

Now throughout all of this I was completely unconcerned at being the possible target of the preacher's disapproval, because I remained confident that the predicted dire consequences of the atheism which kept me out of the Calvinist elect were wholly unfounded and that their picture of humans as totally depraved and sinful, saved only by the explicit grace of God, was one without any foundation in fact, and so of interest only from a sociocultural point of view. I admit that the Calvinist attitude to the individual's unavoidable sinfulness is an extreme case, but many ascetic religions decry the sins of the flesh, including pleasure taken at food, drink, sex or music.

I take the term 'sin' not in a peculiarly Christian sense but in a more general sense meaning actions, character traits or attitudes which contradict or infringe norms laid down by a particular religion. For example, it is sinful for a Jew or a Moslem to eat pork, it is sinful for a Buddhist to eat meat, or a Hindu to eat beef. The Christian doctrine of original sin is a nasty twist on top of this, since it teaches that all humans come preloaded with sin, by virtue of the actions of our ancestors: we are guilty the moment we come into being, simply by being human. Whether we can do anything to counteract this basic inherited deficit by our actions is a matter of debate among different standpoints: the Pelagians for example think our good actions can do something to counteract the deficit, whereas the Augustinian orthodoxy has it that only Divine Grace can turn the bottom line from red to black.

A believer has to worry all the time about whether he/she is being sinful. The more fussy and particular the prohibitions are, the easier it is to be sinful, even without knowing about it. Ignorance of the law is no excuse. For example, in the seventh century in Britain, King Oswiu of Bernicia celebrated Easter according to the computations of Ionan (Celtic) Christians, whereas his Deiran Queen Eanflæd celebrated according to the revised computations of Rome. Not only did this mean that he might be inconveniently celebrating Easter while his wife was fasting for Lent, but that one set of priests would go to hell for getting the date wrong. The disagreement was resolved in favour of Rome by the Synod of Whitby in 664, as narrated by the Venerable Bede, but it's not clear whether the honestly 'mistaken' Ionans were spared the fire or not.

An atheist never needs to worry that something they are doing is sinful, and might have dire consequences in the afterlife. I hope I do not need unduly to stress that this does not mean that anything goes. The idea that morality requires religious underpinning was abandoned by leading philosophers at least two centuries ago, not least by the great Hume. It is only the unenlightened, thoughtless and ignorant who think that because God is dead we can do as we like. I have to say this over and over again because many people, religious and non-religious alike, are under the wholly mistaken impression that without God there can be no ethical system of right and wrong, good and bad. I heartily disagree. Obviously I cannot argue the case here in such a space, where it is not my remit, but I do need to stress it. To be freed of the constraints of religious prohibitions is not to be freed of all constraints whatsoever. So while you are not forbidden to eat pork by religious prohibitions, you may want to consider whether there are ethical arguments against eating it which are independent of religion, for example because of the suffering caused to pigs by current livestock rearing methods, or because keeping livestock diverts food that could be better used to feed the human hungry. Many vegetarians are atheists. I am not a vegetarian, but as a morally responsible human being I am willing to listen to their reasons.

Over the millennia there is no field of human behaviour that has attracted more obsession and fury from religions than sex. Whether, when, how, with whom, and to what purpose have been the subject of intense scrutiny, disagreement, regulation and coercion since the destruction of Sodom and Gomorrah, and probably much earlier, right down to our day. Even in the twenty-first century many religions not only forbid morally neutral sexual practices such as homosexuality, but various religions uphold or promote immoral practices related to sexuality, such as child brides and female genital mutilation (roughly two million procedures a year, according to Amnesty International). In five Moslem countries, namely Saudi Arabia, Iran, Mauritania, Sudan, and Yemen, homosexuality is a capital offence: for example in Iran some 4,000 individuals have been executed for homosexuality since the Islamic revolution. Sexuality is an area in which there certainly are moral norms: if you don't believe me, think on the appalling case of Josef Fritzl, who if you care to remember, kept his own daughter captive for 24 years in a basement of his house, fathering eight children on her, imprisoning three and allowing one negligently to die at three days of age. If what he did wasn't wrong, there really is no morality. So once again, lack of authoritative direction from holy books does not mean that anything goes. On the other hand, from a modern, liberal enlightened point of view, a lot more is morally acceptable than is allowed by most religious prohibitions. In general, religions and the popular imagination make sexual morality loom much larger than it ought to, to such an extent that for many people being immoral is equated with sexual transgressions. It's time we as a species got over our adolescent obsessions and concentrated on morally somewhat more vital and pressing concerns such as war, genocide, political oppression, injustice towards women, intolerance, worker exploitation, corruption, racism, and the destruction of the planet, to name just a few.

The Afterlife

There is no logical necessity requiring that whoever believes in God must believe in an afterlife, or *vice versa*, but the two beliefs are a commonly held package. One of the main levers of religions in ensuring obedience and compliance among their followers is the promise of rewards and threat of punishments in the hereafter. Rewards include going to heaven, whatever that entails. For example the Qur'an (*Surah An-Naba* 78: 31–34) says 'Verily, for the [righteous], there will be a (paradise); gardens and grapeyards; and young full-breasted maidens of equal age; and a full cup (of wine)'. This is expanded in Hadith number 2,562 in the collection known as the *Sunan al-Tirmidhi* which says, 'The least [reward] for the people of Heaven is 80,000 servants and 72 wives, over which stands a dome of pearls, aquamarine and ruby.' Note that in addition to servants and wives the righteous get to enjoy wine, something they are forbidden on earth. The whole thing sounds like an adolescent male's idea of – heaven! What the women and servants get out of the deal is not so clear.

Conversely, those who do the wrong thing in life (or, if you are a Calvinist, those not preselected by God), get the rough end of the stick. The punishments of hell can range from eternal regret at failing to make the celestial cut to the most excruciating bodily tortures, such as being thrown into the Lake of Fire, as in Revelations. Nor is Christ as tolerant as many think: most people will end in hell according to the gospel: Matthew 7:13-14 'Enter ye in at the strait gate: for wide is the gate, and broad is the way, that leadeth to destruction, and many there be which go in thereat: Because strait is the gate, and narrow is the way, which leadeth unto life, and few there be that find it.'

The atheist who denies that there is an afterlife has, as the Australians say, No Worries, at least on this score. They will not suffer eternal torments, perhaps for something for which they are not responsible, like being born before Jesus. They will not enjoy the eternal bliss of the saved either, but they believe that story is as false as the other, so they are not in fact missing out on anything real.

In summary: if you are an atheist, you have no eternal damnation to fear. That can't be bad.

Modern Morality

Although, as I mentioned, philosophers have been pursuing ethics untrammeled by religion for some time, it is always worth stressing that morality should not and objectively can not rest on religion. If the basic metaphysical tenets of religion are false, and there is no divine lawgiver, moral principles have to come from somewhere else. Basically, they have to come from us.[3] Freed of the constraint of religion, we are thereby enabled to put morality on a sound footing for the first time. I do not claim this has been done yet, but it is work in progress amongst philosophers. We do not have to throw the moral baby out with the religious bathwater. Some moral principles advocated by most religions, such as the Golden Rule: 'Do unto others as you would they do unto you', are worth preserving in suitable form. Nor should we confine the sphere of the moral to our actions in regard to other humans. My own moral position, like that of Jeremy Bentham or Peter Singer, is pathocentric: if it can suffer, it figures in moral consideration even if it cannot talk or plan for its future.

It is frequently imagined that every morality will converge on some benign common denominator already found in religion. Don't believe it. The New Testament, for example, upholds discrimination against women, persecution of the mentally ill, heretics, atheists, and unconverted Jews, and supports slavery. The Old Testament is even nastier. These morally unacceptable features of Christianity are exposed at length by the same Franz Buggle mentioned before, and he came to the conclusion that one

---

3. John L. Mackie, *Ethics: Inventing Right and Wrong*, Harmondsworth: Penguin, 1977.

can no longer honestly and morally be a Christian.[4] Similar conclusions can doubtless be drawn from the texts of other religions.

It is then a consolation of atheism that we are able to craft and pursue our morality free of the dictates of pontificating theists of whatever denomination.

The Chief Burden of Atheism

Before I turn to the positive consolations of atheism let me acknowledge that atheism misses out on some of the desirable features of religion. These include not just eternal happiness after death, but a seemingly more abstract but in fact much more important feature: divine restitutive justice. The German philosopher Immanuel Kant argued that the most convincing reason for believing in God and morality is that since the wicked are manifestly not always justly punished in this life, and the good and righteous manifestly not always justly rewarded, there has to be a divine court and just retribution for worldly wrongdoing and reward for worldly rightdoing, to balance the books. An atheist lacks this comforting assurance. An evil drug baron whose accumulated wealth rests on the narcotic destruction of many lives, an evil ruler whose path to power is over the innocent corpses of women and children, may well evade worldly punishment for the duration of their life, and even live in power and luxury. The twentieth century is regrettably prominent in cases of this kind: Adolf Hitler and Joseph Stalin, Mao Zedong and Pol Pot, people in whose responsibility lie the wrongful death and ruin of millions, never got the punishment they deserved. Stalin and Mao died natural deaths. So too did Genghis Khan and the first Chinese emperor Qin Shi Huang, each after causing the deaths of tens or hundreds of thousands in their military campaigns. It is a sad fact that no earthly punishment that could have been inflicted on these individuals would have adequately compensated the amount of suffering they caused. Smaller fry get away scot-free too. Many a murderous concentration camp guard or Stalinist apparatchik died a peaceful death as a respectable

---

4. Franz Buggle, *Denn sie wissen nicht, was sie glauben. Oder warum man redlicherdweise nicht mehr Christ sein kann*, Reinbek: Rowohlt, 1992.

citizen. There are untold numbers of cases. Conversely, the saintly and good may be evilly killed: one need only think of the White Rose, the University of Munich group including students Sophie Scholl and her brother Hans, inspired by their philosophy professor Kurt Huber, who were practically the only open opposition to the war in Germany during World War II. They were arrested, summarily tried and guillotined by the Nazis for merely writing and distributing leaflets that disagreed with the war and criticised the Nazi regime.

In a world without post-death readjustment, the good and innocent may unjustly suffer and the bad and guilty unjustly prosper. It was ever thus and will ever be so. The recognition that there is no compensating system of supernatural justice is in my view the heaviest burden an atheist has to bear by comparison with her believing counterpart. Of course the atheist considers the believer's confidence illusory, and even itself detrimental, since it can weaken the will to seek and implement justice in this life. To say of some misfortune, such as infant death, natural disaster, or accident, 'It is the will of God' is essentially a quietistic motto: it encourages inaction, when in many cases (not all, of course), something can be done. For example, earthquakes are termed even now 'acts of God', but to ward against the loss of life due to earthquakes, earthquake warning systems can be built and civil emergency procedures developed and rehearsed. The thought that Hitler, Stalin and co are burning in hell for their wickedness is no consolation to an atheist, who doesn't believe it. The atheist is thus left to rail, rant and regret that more was not done in this life to impede their evildoings. Since there is no restitutive justice after this life, we have to bend our efforts all the more earnestly to ensuring that as far as possible such justice is meted out in this life.

The Upside of Being an Atheist
Is there any kind of positive consolation that an atheist can claim for herself? There are consolations which are equally available to believers and unbelievers, such as the love of a partner and family, the help and sympathy of friends, the unexpected help of strangers, the realisation that others have suffered similar afflic-

tions before and overcome them. Someone who has suffered bereavement or a broken relationship may well be consoled by the thought that they have seen others come out of their grief and distress, rebuild their lives, move on, put the bad times behind them, and so on. I knew a philosopher who in middle life married a beautiful younger woman and they had a child. The child accidentally fell out of a window and was killed. The mother, stricken with grief, committed suicide on the child's grave. My friend lost his whole family. Yet, though not a religious man, he carried on and died some years later of natural causes, supported by his internal fortitude, the support of friends and colleagues, and his loves of jazz, literature, food, wine, and good philosophy. Whenever I think that something in my life is less than perfect, I think of this colleague, and I am awed and humbled.

There are many aspects of life equally accessible to believers and unbelievers, and which can play a consolatory role: the love and friendship of family and friends, the respect of colleagues, the satisfaction of achievements, the beauty of the arts, the natural world and human beings, the worldly satisfactions of comfort, food and drink, sunlight and sex. The Epicurean philosophers of ancient Greece rightly esteemed such pleasures and satisfactions as conducive to a rich, satisfying and happy life. Further, for an unbeliever their enjoyment is in itself guilt-free.

But now we come to the real issue. Without trying to say how in general an atheist should live her life, about which there are many things to say and many ways to live, since absence of a belief in God tells you precious little positive about how you can or should live, are there any aspects of one's atheistic belief that are positively consoling in times of distress? I think there are. Firstly, there is the fact that the beauty and pleasure we experience in nature, art and with other human beings is a wholly gratuitous good, not the gift of anyone to whom we should be duly thankful. Kant wrote that two things filled him with awe: the starry heavens above him and the moral law within him. I am with him all 50% of the way. Kant lived too early to see the images from the Hubble telescope and appreciate just how beautiful the heavens indeed are. We know that the rich panoply of nature has her awful and destructive side as well, from viral infections to supernovae. As a fundamentally value-free environment, we should not expect anything else from it. Yet we may be increasingly awed by the delicacy of the balance which enables us to live and thrive long enough to appreciate not only nature's show, but also to think and probe beneath the surface and uncover the grounds of that show in science.

And that brings me to the second consolation. Despite humans' depressingly aggressive nature and their inhumanity one to another, about which more than enough has been said and written, we humans are still awe-inspiring creatures: the only beings in the universe to our knowledge to possess language, to engage in the scientific investigation of the universe's structure and regularities, and to appreciate the complexities of that universe. Every week brings new discoveries about the way of the world, and I remain perpetually in awe of and grateful for our ability to accomplish this, despite the many obstacles placed in our way by external and internal nature. Add to this our physical and technological prowess, from the wheel to spaceflight, and our exquisite bodily control, from writing and watchmaking, singing and playing instruments, to skiing and ballet. Finally there is our cornucopia of artistic and imaginative production in the arts, literature, and music. No other creature in the known universe comes anywhere close to our achievements. We may harbour murderers and genocides among our kin, but we also have our Mozarts, Michelangelos and Einsteins: taken overall our powers and achievements are breathtaking.

Finally let me turn to death, that one great unavoidable. It is widely held that religion owes its origin in good part to our terror in the face of death, for as much as bad natural events may be unexpected, they typically give way to others which are less dire, but death is irreversible, and takes each of us. The sadness of the deaths of those who love, the tragedy of those taken young or by accident, disease, crime or war, are part of the fabric of existence of finite organisms such as we are, and there is nothing that a nonbeliever can hope for that matches the believer's (in my view illusory) hope of an afterlife. Yet an atheist can refuse to be despairing in the face of death. A finite life lived in that complex balanced fulfilment that Aristotle calls *eudaimonia* has a rounded beauty like that of a flower or a great melody. It can be inspirational to others, and a source of satisfaction to those who knew the deceased. A person confronting death need not fear it even when they expect no resurrection.

Given that we age and become progressively enfeebled as we do so, in normal circumstances death is not only the inevitable but the socially right thing. We clear a way for those younger ones who come after and have a fresh try. And from a biological point of view, death is nature's way of providing each new generation with fresh organisms facing the challenges of adaptation. Without death there is neither nutrition for others, nor scope for evolution. We are each of us products of an unbroken chain of lives, each previous one of which ended in death, going back to the primal organisms. Whatever else our lineage is, it is a lineage of survivors. So death plays its necessary and positive part in the continuation of life, regrettable or tragic though the passing of an individual may be.

So are we atheists condemned to live a dour miserable life dreading death, or a debauched hedonistic one trying to forget it? The answer is surely 'neither'. The atheist has her pleasures like others, is able to enjoy them without guilt and may indeed savour them more deeply in the knowledge they are all one-off. The atheist faces death as annihilation, whether with equanimity, regret, indifference or welcome, depending on temperament. An atheist is just as well placed as any believer to appreciate the beauty of art and nature, the warmth of love and affection, the wonder of discovery, and the grandeur of the universe. They are equally able to define and live a moral and upright life: whether they do so is another matter.

That reluctant but staunch unbeliever Charles Darwin ends *On the Origin of Species* with the words: 'There is grandeur in this view of life, with its several powers, having been originally breathed into a few forms or into one; and that, whilst this planet has gone cycling on according to the fixed law of gravity, from so simple a beginning endless forms most beautiful and most wonderful have been, and are being, evolved.' Amen.

Reading
The great thing about being a freethinker, as atheists used to be called, is that you are free to think for yourself, without anyone, myself included, telling you what you should think, or read. I will just mention one or two things I like reading. I always enjoy reading and re-reading Bertrand Russell on morality, and I like Richard Dawkins's books on biology, especially *The Ancestor's Tale: A Pilgrimage to the Dawn of Life* (London: Weidenfeld & Nicolson, 2004), though I find his anti-religious writings too abrasive for enjoyment. On why we morally should not be Christians, Russell's pithy comments have been copiously updated by Buggle, if you read German. For more positive suggestions on how to be moral without religion, see the websites of the various humanist organisations. For a couple of consolations I share, see the surprisingly unreligious motto from Schweitzer.

CHAPTER EIGHT

The Consolation of Buddhism

Dónall Mc Ginley

What consolation or benefit might we derive from Buddhist thought? The reason we need consolation is that we suffer, and Buddhism offers an account of the origin of suffering, as well as practical means to overcome it. Buddhism is a spiritual tradition that originated in northern India in the 5th century BCE, with the teachings of the historical Buddha, Siddhartha Gautama (c.490-c.410 BCE) and developed into distinctive schools of thought and practice across the Far East. 'Buddha' means an enlightened or awakened being, and the Buddha's teaching, the Dharma, offers a path to enlightenment and freedom from suffering to those who follow it. At its height, the Buddhist world expanded from India and Sri Lanka to China, Japan, Korea, Burma, Vietnam, Cambodia, Singapore, Thailand, Malaysia, Nepal, Mongolia and Tibet, and to the areas now covered by Indonesia, Pakistan, Afghanistan, and Uzbekistan. India's great Buddhist civilisation came to a violent end with the Islamic invasions which devastated the region between the 8th and 12th centuries. The Buddhist monastic universities such as Nalanda, Odantapuri and Vikramashila were destroyed, the monks killed or scattered to the winds and Buddhist texts burned. The 20th century has seen a return of Buddhism to India, due to in influx of Tibetans fleeing the Chinese communist invasion, as well as a movement towards Buddhism among the oppressed castes of India, in part because of Buddhism's total rejection of the caste system. From around the first century to the 12th century CE there flourished in India a sophisticated scholastic system of Buddhist philosophy belonging to the Mahayana (Great Vehicle) tradition. My focus in this discussion will be mainly on the Mahayana Buddhism that was transmitted from India to Tibet between the 8th and 12th centuries.

There is some debate as to whether Buddhism ought to be

characterised as a religion or as a philosophy. Some describe religion as involving belief in a divine creator. Not only does Buddhism not postulate a first cause, or creator, it is an implication of its metaphysics that there can be no such creator. So according to some scholars Buddhism should be regarded as a philosophy or a spiritual way of life, rather than as a religion. However, given that Buddhist practice includes ceremony and ritual, prayers and devotion, a monastic movement, statues and religious artworks (all anthropological markers of religion), it seems wrong to deny that it is a religion. Moreover, faith is an important component of traditional Buddhist thought and practice. There are limitations to our knowledge, not ourselves being enlightened. So there are Buddhist doctrines that are taken to be subject to rational demonstration, and there are elements that are revealed and are held on faith, being such that only enlightened beings (Buddhas) can know them directly. (The Buddhist belief in past and future lives, and the doctrine of *karma*, the belief that happiness and suffering are caused by past positive and negative actions respectively, are two notable examples of Buddhist doctrines which we are incapable of knowing with certainty in our present state.) What marks someone out as a Buddhist is that they have taken 'refuge' in what Buddhists refer to as 'The Three Jewels': The Buddha (the enlightened one), the Dharma (the teaching of the Buddha) and the Sangha (the spiritual community who practice the Buddha's teachings). The sense of 'refuge' implied here is that of taking refuge in a place of sanctuary with someone who will protect you and look after your best interests.

The Buddhist Worldview

In the West, Buddhism has generated a lot of recent interest and often a great deal of misunderstanding. For instance, in his 1994 book *Crossing the Threshold of Hope*, Pope John Paul II included a chapter on Buddhism in which he highlighted what he took to be its negative or nihilistic attitude to the world, claiming that 'both the Buddhist tradition and the methods deriving from it have an almost exclusively *negative soteriology*'.[1] He continued:

1. John Paul II, *Crossing the Threshold of Hope* (Alfred A. Knopf, 1994) p 85

The 'enlightenment' experienced by Buddha comes down to the conviction that the world is bad, that it is the source of evil and of suffering for man. To liberate oneself from this evil, one must free oneself from this world, necessitating a break with the ties that join us to external reality – ties existing in our human nature, in our psyche, in our bodies. The more we are liberated from these ties, the more we become indifferent to what is in the world, and the more we are freed from suffering, from the evil that has its source in the world.[2]

In the same work he also described Buddhist 'nirvana' (i.e., enlightenment) as 'a state of perfect indifference with regard to the world'.[3]

But nothing could be further from the truth. The response from Buddhists to the Pope's critique of Buddhism was quite telling. For instance, in response to this critique, Tibetan Lama Thinley Norbu wrote:

I am bewildered by the Pope's paradoxical way of openly and obviously insulting Buddhism. Although in one way it is seriously insulting, at the same time, I can see that the Pope has let a good thought suddenly emerge without examining it. Even if he threateningly shakes his sceptre a little, he knows that somehow Buddhism is harmless, which is why he can say anything he wishes about it. So, unnoticeably and unintentionally, the Pope has the positive conception that Buddhism will not hurt anyone.[4]

This brings us to one of the most important tenets of Buddhism, non-violence. The fundamental aim of all Buddhist practice is to free oneself and others from suffering, and the basis of this is, first of all, not harming others or oneself. Buddhism's primary methods are mindfulness, awareness and reason. According to the Buddha, all our suffering has its origin in our attachment to an exaggerated and ultimately false view of a

2. Ibid, pp 85-86
3. Ibid, p 86
4.Thinley Norbu, *Welcoming Flowers, from across the Cleansed Threshold of Hope* (Jewel Publishing House, 1997) p 84

completely independent self; a permanent, autonomous, enduring 'I' or 'me'. Our clinging to this unreal self is the ultimate origin of suffering. The primary tool of Buddhist practice is mindfulness. Without mindfulness it is impossible to practise other Buddhist teachings with consistency. We need to examine the mind all the time. Awareness and mindfulness give us some space to step back and look at our actions without being too caught up in our emotions and in attachment to self which clouds our judgement.

We shouldn't think that the aim of Buddhist teaching is to provide us with pleasing psychological states. The damage done by negative emotions and mental delusions is not merely psychological. We can see the devastating effects of delusional states of mind such as attachment, greed, indifference to others and self-deception, all of which have their origin in the self-cherishing attitude. Recent events such as the war in Iraq and the collapse of the capitalist financial system both have their origins in these delusions.

Before going further I will say something about the overall worldview into which Buddhist philosophy falls. First, on the Buddhist view the universe is not a human-centred thing. Buddhists do not view the world as a platform created for human beings' use; and they have certainly never thought that the world is just a few thousand years old. The universe does not exist for us humans. On the Buddhist view, time extends infinitely far back, without beginning. While this cosmos had a beginning, it was preceded by another, and so on without beginning. Yet Buddhism does view human existence as supremely important and extremely rare. The Buddha told a story about a turtle that lived in a vast ocean. The turtle surfaces for air only once in a hundred years. There is also a wooden yoke floating on that ocean. Now consider how unlikely it would be for the turtle to surface with its head inside the wooden yoke. A human life, claimed the Buddha, is even rarer than that and correspondingly precious.[5]

Secondly, according to Buddhism there is no creator of the universe. The universe has always existed and there is no need to postulate a first cause, and on the Buddhist view, just as the uni-

5. *The Mahayana Mahaparinirvana Sutra*, trs Kosho Yamamoto (1973) revised by Tony Page (Nirvana Publications, 2007) ch 2, p 17

verse has no beginning, our minds too have always existed, without beginning. Our current conscious mind is the product of a previous continuum that stretches back without beginning. One's mind, on this view, is not an enduring, autonomous entity, it is a sequence of conscious states that arise from prior causes; and the mind itself is made up of distinct parts, or aggregates, just as physical objects are made up of parts.

Furthermore, if one accepts the conclusions of Buddhist metaphysics, then there can be nothing like a first cause or a self-subsistent creator because everything that exists depends upon other things for its existence. Everything that exists is a dependently arising entity (this is equivalent to the doctrine that everything lacks inherent existence). Paul Williams, an English scholar of Buddhist philosophy, recently argued that even if Buddhists do not believe that the world had a beginning in time, Buddhism has no answer to the question: 'Why is there something rather than nothing?'[6] Surely, the argument goes, even if there always has been a world it is still possible that such a world might never have existed. So Buddhist thought leaves the question of why there is something rather than nothing unanswered, whereas the theist can point to God as the answer. However, it is not open to the theist to give an answer to this question either. The question is such that it demands an explanation for absolutely everything there is, and because of this there is nothing we can appeal to which is outside of what we demand an explanation for. Even if there is a creator the question 'why is there something rather than nothing?' applies as much to it as to anything else. So the question itself is a bad philosophical question; it is necessarily unanswerable. If it shows us anything it is that the demand for an answer to this total question, which asks for an explanatory account of absolutely everything, is a mistake. (It is noteworthy that the great Christian scholastics of the Middle Ages never posed the question in the aforementioned form, they asked for an explanation for contingent events, not for absolutely everything that exists.)

Given the Buddhist view that the universe has always existed, we might ask whether its existence has some purpose. Is there a

---

6. Paul Williams, *The Unexpected Way*, (T & T Clark, 2002) pp 27-33

meaning of life on this view? Not really! Purposes and meanings are assigned to things by minds. So while life has great import-ance and value, it does not have a purpose beyond what purpose we ourselves give it (any more than, say, matter or space have a meaning or a purpose).

The Four Noble Truths and The Two Truths
The historical Buddha, Siddhartha Gautama, is said to have reached complete enlightenment while meditating under a tree in Bodh Gaya in northern India some 2,500 years ago. Enlightenment, or *Nirvana*, is complete knowledge of the nature of reality and complete freedom from *samsara* (the cycle of suffering and rebirth).

The first teaching given by the Buddha after his enlighten-ment concerned the 'Four Noble Truths'.[7] These are:
1. The Truth of Suffering
2. The Truth of the Origin of Suffering
3. The Truth of the Cessation of Suffering
4. The Truth of the Path to Freedom from Suffering

The first truth we need to recognise is the reality of suffering: that we and other living beings suffer, that the world is unsatis-factory because of suffering. Unless we recognise this truth, we will not attempt to free ourselves or others from suffering. Secondly, the Buddha identified the origin of suffering as an in-nate ignorance, our misperception of an enduring, autonomous, fixed self. This innate grasping at a (non-existent) independent self (an 'I' or 'me') is the fundamental delusion from which anger, hatred and irrational attachment follow. The root of suffering is our ignorance, a fundamental, innate misconception of reality (grasping at self). From this source we generate irrational attach-ment to ourselves, to our possessions, to pleasures that are after all impermanent. This innate ignorance keeps us bound up in *sam-sara*, the beginningless cycle of rebirths. The third noble truth is that it is possible to free oneself from the suffering of *samsara*. The fourth noble truth is that there is a path that can lead us away to

7. 'Setting in Motion the Wheel of Truth', in *The Book of Protection*, trs Piyadassi Thera (Buddhist Publication Society, 1999) pp 74-79

this cessation of suffering; this was the path which the Buddha himself had followed and completed. The Buddha identified the path to liberation from suffering and to complete enlightenment. This path has two aspects: developing wisdom (awareness of the interdependent nature of reality) and developing morality, helping others and performing only non-violent, non-harming actions.

In Buddhism (as in many schools of western philosophy) there is a distinction between appearance and reality. But what Buddhists call the Two Truths, ultimate truth and conventional truth, do not correspond precisely with the appearance/reality distinction found in western philosophy. On the Buddhist view, everything in the world has two distinct 'modes of existence',[8] conventional existence and ultimate existence. The ultimate reality, on the Buddhist view, is 'emptiness' (shunyata), i.e. the absence of an enduring, autonomous self (both for persons and for all other phenomena). In other words, things lack inherent existence. Conventional reality refers to the way the world is relative to our minds; but on the level of conventional reality there is also a distinction between how things seem to us and how they really are. So from the conventional point of view we can still misperceive aspects of the world, believing things to exist truly independently (rather than as dependent arisings). We are also unaware of other facets of conventional reality, such as the phenomena of rebirth and karma, very subtle aspects of reality to which our minds do not yet have direct access.

According to this theory, ultimate reality is not a positive, substantial phenomenon; it is a kind of negation, the absence of a particular kind of nature. Emptiness does not mean nothingness or non-existence. (Such a view would not only be rather self-defeating, but is obviously false.) The Middle Way (Madhyamaka) school of Mahayana Buddhism holds that emptiness is equivalent to 'dependent arising'. Saying that things lack an inherent, autonomous or permanent reality means just that they exist in

8. The Dalai Lama, *Transcendent Wisdom: A Commentary on the Ninth Chapter of Shantideva's* Guide to the Bodhisattva's Way of Life, (Snow Lion Publications, 1988) p 21

dependence upon other things (causes and conditions, their integral parts and in dependence upon the mind that perceives them).

Karma and Rebirth
Buddhist teachings are essentially practical. The primary aim of Buddhist teachings is to free living beings from suffering rather than to engage in metaphysical speculation. As an illustration of the view that practical action is more important than metaphysical speculation, the Buddha told the following story.

> There is a man who has been struck by a poisoned arrow. His relatives call in a doctor to relieve him of the poison and mean to extract the arrow. The man says: 'Don't touch me for a moment! I shall think: From where did such an arrow come? Who discharged it? ...What type of wood is this? Bamboo or willow? ... What bird does the feather of the arrow come from? Is it from a crow, an owl, or an eagle?'[9]

As interesting as these questions might be, what one should be concerned about is removing the arrow and getting healthy again. Similarly, on the Buddhist view, our response to our current suffering should be to do something practical to alleviate it. Many Buddhist teachings are described as being 'skilful means' (*upaya*, in Sanskrit), techniques employed for a specific purpose. These are methods and ways of thinking that, while they may not accurately reflect how the world really is, are useful for developing awareness, compassion or wisdom. Skilful means can also involve interim or provisional views that work as antidotes to specific problems, lessening delusional states of mind. So, for instance, to lessen excessive attachment to one's body one can consider that the body contains blood and guts, which we would generally regard as impure. This is purely a temporary means to decreasing attachment; we should not mistake it for being an accurate description of how the world really is, because in reality the body is not impure.

9. *The Mahayana Mahaparinirvana Sutra*, trs Kosho Yamamoto (1973) revised by Tony Page (Nirvana Publications, 2007) ch 21, pp 208-209

While the Buddha advised against speculation for its own sake, Buddhism does offer an account of the origin of our suffering, an account of *samsara* (the cycle of uncontrolled rebirth) and of *karma* (the law of cause and effect that binds us in this cycle of rebirth). After all, in order to alleviate suffering we need to know its source and how to cut it off at its source. According to the theory of *karma*, good and bad things happen to us as a result of past good and bad actions, in this and in previous lives. Our harmful actions will result in suffering (and an unfortunate rebirth) and our good actions will result in happiness (and a fortunate rebirth). The Indian master Atisha (c.980-1054 CE), who taught widely in Tibet, said:

> If the root is poisonous, the stem, the branches and the leaves will be poisonous. If the root is medicinal, the stem, the branches, and the leaves will also be medicinal.[10]

Negative actions will have negative results, and positive actions will have positive results. Positive actions will result in happiness for ourselves and others, whereas negative actions will result in suffering for ourselves and others. But if we only consider this life, then the account of this origin of suffering is impossible to defend. Good people suffer terribly and innocents live lives of torment, while cruel, greedy and vicious people flourish and attain great status and power. The theory of *karma* can only be considered plausible (as a universal explanation for suffering) if there are past and future lives, and we might well demand independent reasons to suppose that there are past and future lives. The theory of *karma* appears to stem in part from a belief in the infallibility of the law of cause and effect and, further to this, that effects will be of the same kind as the cause. So good actions have good effects for the agent and bad actions will have bad effects. Similarly, a state of consciousness can only be caused by a prior state of consciousness and cannot be the result of some non-conscious process. In this way the belief that causes are similar in

10. Cited in Chökyi Dragpa, *Uniting Wisdom and Compassion: Illuminating the Thirty-Seven Practices of a Bodhisattva*, trs Heidi I. Köppl (Wisdom Publications, 2004) p 63

kind to their effects is used as a justification for belief in rebirth and for the world's existing without beginning and without end. Looking at it another way, the theory of *karma* implies that all causation is, at bottom, *moral* causation, and this would be disputed by many people.

Some Buddhists do not profess a strong belief in rebirth, or it does not feature prominently in their worldview. Agnosticism about rebirth is common in the Zen tradition, as well as among western Buddhists. Even some Tibetan lamas treat *karma* primarily as a 'skilful means' towards an end, a useful way to think of things in order to lessen our attachment to good situations and revulsion towards bad situations, and our resultant anger and resentment. Using the framework of *karma* one can perhaps look upon situations with greater equanimity, and so respond less rashly and with more wisdom. The theory of *karma* also entails that no action is insignificant. Every action, however apparently trivial, will have effects. Such a view will surely contribute to an attitude of mindfulness towards one's actions. It is also worth pointing out that the earliest Buddhist schools, making up the *Theravada* tradition, unlike many in the *Mahayana* tradition, hold that *karma* is only one causal mechanism amongst others, rather than being a universal explanation.

It must be said that a good deal of the Buddhist path, traditionally described, relies on past and future lives and on the notion of purification of bad *karma* and the accumulation of positive merit, as being essential to the path. If we do not undergo uncontrolled rebirth then *samsara* (cyclic existence) is not something we will have to overcome. Likewise, the supreme motivation of *bodhichitta*, the commitment to become enlightened in order to free sentient beings from *samsara*, relies on the reality of rebirth. The enlightenment described by the Buddha means an end to uncontrolled rebirth, the total cessation of suffering, and omniscience, and is the result of direct realisation of emptiness motivated by the wish to free all sentient beings from *samsara*. Clearly, if rebirth is rejected this view of enlightenment cannot be maintained.

Karma is often described as being the foundation of Buddhist morality. However, it seems to me, rather, that the law of *karma* mirrors what is known in western philosophy as the 'natural law'. The basis of morality is in the nature of suffering and harm and in our natural relations to other beings. What makes an act wrong is that it causes suffering and what makes an act good is that it promotes well-being. What makes an act of mine that promotes someone's well-being a good act is not that I will myself derive some benefit from it in the future. What makes a harmful act wrong is simply that it causes harm, not that it will rebound on the agent at some future time. We do not need punishment and reward for morality to have a foundation (neither punishment and reward by God, nor by a universe governed by the law of *karma*).

The reason we ought to perform good actions is that they are good, not because we will benefit from them. However, it is the case that the lives of those who cause a great deal of harm are rightly regarded as impoverished in some way, whereas those who are kind and compassionate tend to live more worthwhile lives, they are nicer people, more humane and more admirable human beings.

Compassion, Emptiness and Meditation

In Buddhism our motivation for action is also centrally important in assessing its moral value. An act that benefits someone which is performed out of self-interest, or done begrudgingly, is less meritorious than if it were done out of a pure motivation. The greatest motivation, from the Buddhist perspective, is *bodhichitta* (the wish and intention to achieve enlightenment in order to benefit all living beings). The foundation for *bodhichitta* is great compassion, compassion that extends to all living beings, including animals and beings from realms of existence outside our own. This compassion is the sincere wish to free every living being from suffering. *Bodhichitta* and direct realisation of emptiness are the requirements for achieving enlightenment. One who has achieved *bodhichitta* is called a *Bodhisattva*.

In the final dedication from *A Guide to the Bodhisattva's Way of Life*, written in the 8th century CE by Shantideva, a philosopher from the monastic university of Nalanda, we find a statement of a Bodhisattva's motivation:

For as long as space endures
And for as long as living beings remain,
Until then may I too abide
To dispel the misery of the world.[11]

The Dalai Lama writes:

Genuine freedom and liberation can only be achieved when our fundamental ignorance, our habitual misapprehension of the nature of reality, is totally overcome. This ignorance, which underlies all our emotional and cognitive states, is the root factor that binds us to the perpetual cycle of life and death in Samsara.[12]

According to Buddhist doctrine, our minds have an innate predisposition to misapprehend or misperceive the way things actually are. How do we come to perceive things correctly, thus removing a major source of suffering for ourselves and others? Philosophy has its place, but an intellectual understanding of emptiness will not really change our natural dispositions, our innate grasping at self. In the Buddhist path meditation is central. Lama Panchen Ötrul Rinpoche describes the mind as being like a rubber band, when we pull it in one direction it quickly returns to its original position.[13] Through meditation the mind becomes more flexible and we can learn to be less selfish and more compassionate, and over time our minds will no longer return automatically to their habitual, self-clinging state. The biologist Richard Dawkins has stated that human beings are now in a position to transcend the somewhat violent, brutal natures bestowed on us by evolution, (because we have self-awareness, sympathy and reason.) The truth of Darwinian evolution does not entail that human societies must be based on greed and pure self-interest;

11. Shantideva, *A Guide to the Bodhisattva's Way of Life*, tr, Stephen Batchelor (Library of Tibetan Works and Archives, 1979) ch 10, verse 55, p 193
12. The Dalai Lama, *The World of Tibetan Buddhism: An Overview of Its Philosophy and Practice*, (Wisdom Publications, 1995) p 10
13. From a teaching given at Jampa Ling Tibetan Buddhist Centre, Co Cavan, in 2004

Dawkins believes that 'what makes humans special is their ability to transcend naked Darwinism.'[14] Arguably, the techniques and teachings of Buddhist meditation give us a clear method for doing just this. It is a practical means to acting less selfishly, less destructively and more altruistically. Human behaviour is often all too like that of the aggressive chimpanzee, but unlike our violent cousins we have the ability to change the way we think and act. Ani Tenzin Palmo, a Tibetan Buddhist nun from England who spent over twelve years in solitary meditation in a Himalayan cave, writes, 'When people cannot control their behaviour, it is because they cannot control their minds.'[15] Taking responsibility for our actions is an important step towards acting responsibly. The tendency in modern society to blame others for one's own free actions is at the root of the extreme recklessness that causes of much suffering in the world. All Buddhist teachings have the primary aim of benefiting sentient beings, and the main purpose of Buddhist practice is taming and training the mind, purifying our delusional attitudes and cultivating wisdom and compassion. Delusions such as anger, hatred, attachment, jealousy and greed are the result of self-cherishing. However, these delusions that result from an innate misperception of ourselves and our world are not our nature (although they might seem to be, given how ingrained they are and how easily negative emotions arise). These causes of suffering are not permanent because we are able to remove them. Eliminating the causes of suffering will result in a complete cessation of suffering.

According to Buddhism, all living beings have a 'Buddha Nature', an innate potential for enlightenment. Our innate self-clinging attitude is not our real nature because we can change it. Our fundamental nature is pure and perfect, but it is obscured by the mistaken view that grasps at self. We can free ourselves from samsara permanently, by removing the grasping at self that is its root. This is achieved by generating wisdom.

Shantideva wrote:

14. Marek Kohn, 'To Rise Above', in Richard Dawkins, *How a Scientist Changed the Way We Think*, eds Alan Grafen & Mark Ridley (Oxford University Press, 2006) p 250
15. Ani Tenzin Palmo, *Reflections on a Mountain Lake: Teachings on Practical Buddhism* (Snow Lion Publications, 2002) p 122

All of these practices were taught
By the Buddha for the sake of wisdom.
Therefore those who wish to pacify suffering
Should generate this wisdom.[16]

Buddhist meditation takes many distinct forms, all of which fall into one of two categories: Calm Abiding Meditation (*Samatha* in Sanskrit) and Insight Meditation (*Vipasyana* in Sanskrit). In calm abiding the mind rests single-pointedly on an object of meditation. The most common kind of calm abiding meditation is focusing on the breath. Insight meditation includes analytical meditations, as well as various kinds of introspective meditation; meditation on emptiness falls into this category. Buddhist meditations include looking at thoughts as they arise and fall away without grasping onto them, looking at the luminous nature of the mind itself and at its ultimate nature. Also there are meditations on the preciousness of human life, on death, on developing compassion and equanimity and on emptiness (the ultimate nature of persons and of phenomena). There are also the complex Tantric meditations of *Vajrayana* Buddhism (the diamond vehicle) that involve visualisation and the various yogas that harness subtle energies in the body (*transforming* negative emotions into positive qualities) and developing very clear states of mind which can then be turned to investigate the nature of the mind itself. In addition to formal meditation, the meditator must learn to integrate his or her awareness into everyday life.

On the Buddhist view, we can discern the nature of the mind and of reality through introspection. In the meditation on selflessness or emptiness we search inwardly for the 'self', the 'I' which we grasp onto, the enduring, autonomous subject of our happiness and suffering, our thoughts and emotions, the owner of our property, etc. Can we locate this self? Is the self my body or my mind? The self does not seem to have parts; it is unitary, simple, autonomous and unchanging. No matter how much we search for it, we cannot find it. We gain knowledge of ultimate reality first indirectly through reasoning and then directly through

16. Shantideva, *A Guide to the Bodhisattva's Way of Life*, trs Stephen Batchelor (Library of Tibetan Works and Archives, 1979) ch 9, v 1, p 136

meditation. Once emptiness is experienced, the meditator rests in this non-conceptual awareness.

The Middle Way (*Madhyamaka*) school of *Mahayana* Buddhist philosophy originated with the philosopher-monk Nagarjuna (2nd century CE) and his interpretation of the *Perfection of Wisdom* sutras. According to this view, emptiness (*shunyata*), the ultimate nature of reality, is understood as a 'middle way' between the two extremes; the extreme of holding that things exist absolutely of themselves and the extreme nihilism. The first extreme is believing that things exist in the way they appear to us to exist, as autonomous, independent, enduring things. This view is the innate perception of independent selves that binds us in *samsara*. However, when we try to establish that things really do have this solid, independent existence we find that this world of self-existing things is illusory. It is possible to misunderstand the implications of emptiness, this lack of inherent existence, thinking that it negates conventional reality completely. This 'nihilist' view denies the valid existence of the everyday world and of conventional realities such as operation of cause and effect. If one thinks that the emptiness of persons and other phenomena implies that nothing exists at all, or that moral values are make-believe, then one has fallen into the extreme of nihilism. We must not think that every kind of existence is negated by the reasoning that establishes emptiness.

The Middle Way view is that on the ultimate level of reality things lack any self-sufficient, independent or absolute existence, but that nevertheless they do exist conventionally, in a non-arbitrary and functional way. If we neglect the Buddhist teaching of the Two Truths, that there are two (distinct but inseparable) levels of reality, the ultimate and the conventional, and that everything that exists has these two modes of existence, we will fail to understand emptiness correctly.

The Tibetan philosopher-yogi Je Tsongkhapa (1357-1419) discussed the correct understanding of emptiness in terms of gaining a correct understanding of '*the object to be negated*',[17] i.e. the kind of

---

17. Nam-kha Pel, *Mind Training Like the Rays of the Sun*, trs Brian Beresford, ed Jeremy Russell (Library of Tibetan Works and Archives, 1992) p 111

self-existent, autonomous, independent entity negated by the state of mind perceiving emptiness. Emptiness is not an indistinct absence and it is not nothingness. Only a certain way of existing is negated, not existence *per se*. The meditator must be careful not to negate too much or too little, so as to avoid falling into one or other of the extremes. Conventionally things do exist, but they do not have inherent existence. They exist in dependence on causes and conditions. Emptiness then is equivalent to dependent arising.

There are broadly three kinds of dependent arising, according to Je Tsongkhapa:
1. Things come into being in dependence upon causes and conditions.
2. Things depend for their existence on their parts and the structure of these parts.
3. Things (including ourselves) exist in dependence upon being conceptualised. Things obtain their unity, their identity and their very existence from being mentally labelled, or named. Of themselves, things do not have an independent reality. So the conventional world, the world as it appears to us, is dependent on mental labelling, on thought, for its existence.

When we analyse things looking for an independent identity we cannot find it. While things are empty of inherent existence, they are not utterly non-existent, and they can have effects. In *The Wheel of Sharp Weapons*, an Indian mind-training text, we find an illustration of this:

> When musicians are playing a beautiful melody,
> Should we examine the sound they are making
> We would see that it does not exist by itself.
> But when we are not making our formal analysis,
> Still there is a beautiful tune to be heard,
> Which is merely a label on notes and on players –
> That is why lovely music can lighten sad hearts.[18]

18. Dharmarakshita, *The Wheel of Sharp Weapons*, trs Geshe Ngawang Dhargyey *et al*, (Library of Tibetan Works and Archives, 2nd edition 1994) v 112, p 26

According to the Middle Way interpretation, emptiness and dependent arising are equivalent. In order to check that our interpretation of emptiness is correct we can compare our interpretation of the absence of inherent existence with the view that everything that exists is a dependently arising thing; if the two coincide then our interpretation is correct.

This Middle Way presentation of emptiness is the dominant one in Tibetan Buddhism today. But it is important to note that even within this view there are many subtly differing interpretations. The topic of emptiness is the most profound and most complex in Buddhist philosophy and it has generated a vast scholastic literature that would take many lifetimes to study fully. There are also other schools of thought concerning emptiness within the Buddhist tradition. Anyone studying the Zen Buddhist tradition, for instance, will encounter a quite different view of emptiness, coming from the Mind Only (*Cittamattra*) School of *Mahayana* philosophy which originated with the Indian master Asanga (4th century CE). According to this view, the ultimate reality is mind, and what is negated by the wisdom perceiving ultimate reality is the real distinction between oneself and others. Consciousness, devoid of the distinction between subject and object or self and other, is the ultimate reality. Even though these different interpretations of emptiness contradict one another, they are still considered a valid means to gaining a direct realisation of ultimate reality, which is the ultimate purpose of the teaching.

The wisdom conceiving emptiness is a non-conceptual, direct experience of ultimate reality. This does not mean that it has no content or that it is a vacant experience, nor does it mean that we cannot form concepts about it. For instance, although my experience of the colour blue is non-conceptual, it has content and it can be described using concepts. So the wisdom realising emptiness does not make the world disappear. It is not as if meditation destroys the self – we just come to see that the self does not exist in the way we thought. We see the world as it is (as dependently arising) rather than as consisting in a set of independent, autonomous, enduring persons and things. In a world where we realise that things do not have an inherent self, we will not grasp onto the self and will not be troubled by delusional states of mind that arise from this grasping at self. Things appear to us to exist independently, but in reality they do not.

The Value of Buddhist Thought

We can see that happiness and contentment do not depend exclusively on external circumstances, one's state of mind is much more important. Even rich people are often dissatisfied, though clearly we do need external factors in order to live with dignity. But we would not want to swap our lives with those who make a fortune exploiting the poor and the vulnerable. Who would want to become that kind of person?

Buddhism has a great deal to contribute to those who do not share fully in its worldview. The Buddha did not demand that others blindly accept his teachings. The Buddha said:

> Do not accept my teachings merely out of respect for me, but analyse and check them the way that a goldsmith analyses gold, by rubbing, cutting and melting it.[19]

American-born Tibetan Buddhist nun Thubten Chodron writes:

> I believe that spiritual practice is more about holding questions than finding answers. Seeking one correct answer often comes from a wish to make life – which is basically fluid – into something certain and fixed.[20]

At the very least, an acquaintance with Buddhist thought will allow us to think in a way that perhaps we have never thought before, exposing our minds to an alternative view of reality and of the possibilities for human society. According to the Buddhist view, it is folly to expect peace to result from violence, or universal wellbeing from selfishness and greed. The teachings on interdependence show that the idea that one can really benefit from

19. From *A Sutra on [Pure Realms] Spread Out in a Dense Array*, quoted in Thubten Chodron, *Open Heart, Clear Mind* (Snow Lion Publications, 1990) p 17
20. Thubten Chodron, *Buddhism for Beginners* (Snow Lion Publications, 2001) p 9

another's suffering is ultimately misguided. We humans need not act out of selfishness, and we can expand the circle of our concern beyond ourselves and those with whom we are acquainted. Indeed, human history (which is noted for its brutality) has many examples of the attitude of universal responsibility advocated by Buddhists. Think of the mediaeval movements to elevate the suffering of the poor (including free medical treatment for poor people in monastic hospitals), or the anti-slavery movement of the 18th and 19th centuries. In our own time we have the international human rights movement, the movement for the humane treatment of animals, and the movement against the arms-trade. All these groups of people exhibit the same wide scope of ethical concern and compassionate action. Actor and writer Peter Ustinov said he disliked it when people described small positive acts in the face of great evil as 'a drop of water on a hot tile', which implies that they are ultimately worthless. He preferred to think of them as 'a drop in the ocean'.[21] If the Buddhist view is right then no action is insignificant. Buddhism has also developed a very comprehensive set of meditative practices that can help people realise the most profound possibilities of human nature: awareness, selflessness, compassion and wisdom. These techniques are a means for people to change themselves, and therefore the world, for the better, realising their basic nature.

On the Buddhist view, compassion and wisdom are mutually supporting. As our experience of wisdom perceiving emptiness increases so does our capacity for love and compassion, for selflessness. Likewise, compassion and altruism increase our realisation of the interdependent nature of reality and, therefore, our capacity for realising emptiness. Direct realisation of emptiness is impossible without great compassion. The more we come to realise that everything in the world including ourselves is a dependently arising thing, the more we realise that the idea that our well-being is independent of others' well-being is an illusion. On the *Mahayana* Buddhist view, all good qualities, such as compassion, sympathy, kindness and wisdom, arise in dependence upon others. What we need to survive is provided by others and we should

21. From a BBC television interview

realise their kindness. I will end with a remark from The Dalai Lama:

> If the self had intrinsic identity, it would be possible to speak in terms of self-interest in isolation from that of others. But given that this is not so, given that self and others can only be understood in terms of relationship, we see that self-interest and the interests of others are similarly interrelated. Indeed, within this picture of dependently originated reality, we see that there is no self-interest completely unrelated to others' interests. Due to the fundamental interconnectedness which lies at the heart of reality, your interest is also my interest. Thus my happiness is to a large extent dependent on yours.[22]

22. The Dalai Lama, *Ancient Wisdom, Modern World: Ethics for a New Millennium*, (1999) pp 47-48

Recommended Further Reading

The Dalai Lama, *Ancient Wisdom, Modern World: Ethics for a New Millennium,* (Little, Brown and Company, 1999)

The Dalai Lama, *Awakening the Mind, Lightening the Heart: Core Teachings of Tibetan Buddhism,* (Thorsons, 1997)

Rupert Gethin, *The Foundations of Buddhism,* (OUP, 1998)

John Daido Loori, *Finding the Still Point: A Beginner's Guide to Zen Meditation,* (Shambhala Publications, 2007)

Maura 'Soshin' O'Halloran, *Pure Heart, Enlightened Mind: The Zen Journal and Letters of an Irish Woman in Japan,* (Thorsons, 1994)

Susan Piver, *Quiet Mind: A Beginner's Guide to Meditation,* (Shambhala Publications, 2008)

Shunryu Suzuki, *Zen Mind, Beginner's Mind,* (Weatherhill, 1970)

Ani Tenzin Palmo, *Reflections on a Mountain Lake: Teachings on Practical Buddhism,* (Snow Lion Publications, 2002)

Thubten Chodron, *Buddhism for Beginners,* (Snow Lion Publications, 2001)

Geshe Tsultrim Gyeltsen, *Mirror of Wisdom: Teachings on Emptiness,* (Thubten Dhargye Ling Publications, 2000)

PDF version available free here:

http://www.lamayeshe.com/index.php?sect=article&id=464

Lama Yeshe Losal, *Living Dharma,* (Dzalendara Publications, 2001)

CHAPTER NINE

The Consolation of Craft

Joseph McLoughlin

Why should an economic downturn lead to an interest in philosophy rather than any other subject? The idea may be that the study of philosophy offers the hope of consolation in an economic downturn, some comfort in the wake of financial misfortune. But why, one might ask, should philosophy be of particular importance in offering comfort in such circumstances? Perhaps one's difficulties are such that 'battening down the hatches' or searching for a new way to manage one's finances or a hitherto unexplored business opportunity do not strike one as relevant. After all, an interest in accounting would anyway be better advised in such cases, and a response in practical, financial terms would be more likely to assuage concerns. One presumes, therefore, that practical or material comfort is not sought. This, though, seems a strange response to an economic crises; for if the discomfort is material, would it not make sense to seek a material remedy or material consolation? The peculiarity of a turn to philosophy, it seems, may appeal because one's financial difficulties have been the occasion of a personal crisis such that one hopes in a new approach to life. It is not just that one wishes to assuage one's mind in the face of financial difficulties but that one is calling into question the point of continuing to lead one's life in the same terms. In short, one considers that reconsideration of fundamental aspects of one's life is called for and hopes philosophy may offer practical, substantive steps in a positive direction. The desired consolation is the comfort to be gained from taking the opportunity to putting right fundamental problems.

Why, though, should one think of philosophy as the appropriate response to a personal crisis? Religion, psychoanalysis and art come to mind as subjects that may enable new approaches to life. Religion might be considered the obvious port of call when one feels that a material response to personal difficulties is felt as inadequate; the bread and butter of psychoanalysis is an experienced lack of self-understanding to which material comfort or discomfort is of little consequence. Art, funnily enough, bears one or two striking parallels with philosophy. One may be described legitimately as an 'artist' or a 'philosopher' in the absence of any formal induction or training – unlike for example 'scientist', 'economist', or 'accountant'. One will be a certain kind of philosopher or artist, of course, but legitimately described as a philosopher or artist all the same. The parallels with philosophy are also striking in terms of a popular contrast between 'real' artists or philosophers versus mere 'craftsmen' or, in a phrase coined by one philosopher, 'philosophical labourers'. At a distance, at least, art and philosophy offer the hope of an individualistic, personal activity, in which one may engage outside of any regimented organisation. A strong part of the appeal of both subjects is that they have the air that a fundamental overhaul of one's personal life may begin from an individualistic starting point

In recognising an initial appeal of art and philosophy, however, should one assume that either of these subjects enables practical, substantive answers to questions raised in reconsideration of fundamental aspects of one's life? One popular conception of art is that it is a personal exploration of one's emotions. If this is so, it might seem that it would therefore be very useful in facilitating substantive answers. In fact, one philosopher, R. G. Collingwood conceived of art primarily in terms of artistic activity along these lines. In a nutshell, his conception of artistic activity was that the artist addresses their own emotions and says 'I want to get this clear' (*Principles of Art*, p 114). Collingwood conceived of artistic activity as essentially a process of psychological self-investigation, in which one moved from an opaque consciousness of one's emotions to a 'lucid' or 'intelligible' one (which he idiosyncratically referred to as 'expression'). The physical work of art he considered of secondary importance, the real work of art in his view existed in the artist's imagination – in the way a tune may exist in its composer's mind – and was a vehicle for this process of self-clarification of emotion. For the audience, the physical work of art was a means of reconstructing the artist's emotion in their own minds. If one were considering turning to the individual pursuit of art to offer comfort through enabling one to address fundamental personal concerns, clearly one might think that an investigation of one's emotions along these lines to be a fruitful starting point.

However, while self-clarification of emotions may very well be a good thing in a crisis, what is there to say that art is especially suited to it? After all, religion and psychoanalysis offer personal insight and that's without discussing the merits of long walks, gardening or a few cups of tea. In other words, it is tempting to accept that art along the lines of Collingwood's conception of it is a way of investigating one's emotions and, more broadly, fundamental concerns. But is it? In a way that is not accidental, that one might not just as well have gained from that good walk not to mention the cups of tea? Is there, that is to say, any thing peculiar about art in this regard or is it perhaps just a question of personal luck whether one achieves such insight from engaging in it? In considering a subject for the promise it suggests of consolation in the sense explained, one would like to have a reasonable grounds in advance — and this is where philosophy comes back in — that there is something about art that recommends it as peculiarly suited to this role.

Philosophy comes back in here because an important understanding of philosophy is that of 'philosophy of –.' A large number of the titles of philosophy books available today allude to the philosophy of something or other. But what does it amount to say the 'philosophy of –.' Well, it simply means that philosophy consists in examining and clarifying concepts and practices in a given subject, assessing their intelligibility, relevance and application. For example, while an artist may paint a picture, the philosopher of art, rather than engaging in painting, might ask what is it about pictures that allows them to represent objects or events or people? The philosopher of psychology, rather than engaging in experiments or attempting to discover new psychological laws, might ask, for example, whether the concept of the psychological should be restricted to items, such as beliefs and desires, of which one is conscious or allow unconscious items as well? The philosopher of language, rather than engaging in translation or linguistic studies, might ask about the concept of meaning used in translation and linguistics. Now, there is a two-way street here: conceptual issues influence the way in which practical activity is conducted, and practical activity influences the way in which conceptual questions are posed. So philosophical investigation is not independent of practical engagement with or knowledge of the subject in question. The basic point, however, is that in philosophy one concentrates not on actually producing art, or psychological results or linguistic theories but in examining the concepts and practices implicit in such fields. On this conception of philosophy, the notion that one could turn to philosophy for consolation in the face of a personal crisis occasioned by an economic crisis invites the question 'philosophy of what?' One will not therefore simply turn to philosophy, but will turn to philosophy in turning to some other subject for consolation. As indicated above, the philosophy of art articulated by R. G. Collingwood is particularly suggestive in relation to consolation in the light of a personal crisis. The benefit of philosophy lies in subjecting this view to some scrutiny, to test whether it really supports a recommendation in favour of art as a conduit for clarification of one's emotions and broader personal concerns.

1.The Relationship of Art and Craft

It is in his book, *The Principles of Art,* that Collingwood argues at length for his view that art is essentially the psychological self-investigation of the artist; he argues for a distinction between 'art proper' (*passim*) and craft. He holds that understanding art in terms of craft has inspired a technical theory of art that misrepresents art as essentially technical skill rather than self-clarification of emotion. The understanding of 'art' in terms of craft originates with Plato and Aristotle, who conceived of the poet or artist as a craftsman. In *The Republic* Plato explicitly describes the poet or artist as a craftsman and Aristotle's *Poetics* is largely a technical manual; it comprises principles and rules for the construction of imitations of life, such as epic poetry, tragedies, comedies among other forms. For example, Aristotle explains that differences between forms of poetry, by which he includes drama, arise in virtue of the subject-matter: '… tragedy parts company with comedy, since comedy prefers to imitate persons who are worse, tragedy persons who are better' (p 46). Collingwood argues that over-emphasis of the importance of craft has resulted in the spread of 'art falsely so called' (*passim*). Some typical and obvious kinds of work opposed by Collingwood on the grounds that they are merely 'art falsely so called' because they are just technical exercises are thrillers, whodunnits, weepies, and realistic painting. From the point of view of whether art may be recommended as a vehicle of consolation, much hinges on whether Collingwood succeeds in maintaining the distinction. Remember, the question is not whether someone may happen to gain self-clarification of emotion from art – that would simply leave it as a question of hit-and-miss; rather, the question is whether there is something peculiar to the nature of art that cannot but involve the self-clarification of emotion by the participants. The problem that the concept of craft, or skill, poses is that possession of a craft or skill is indifferent to one's emotional life and one's degree of consciousness of it. Therefore, if the concept of craft is centrally important to the concept of art this counts against thinking that art is peculiarly suited to self-clarification of emotion.

Collingwood describes the notion of craft as the principle 'distorting agent' (p 107) in analyses of the notion of art; he holds that it is the root idea giving rise to various kinds of art 'falsely so called' and considers it to stand in the way of a 'sound aesthetic' (p 16). While his discussion ranges over a number of features associated with the notion of craft, he identifies the core idea in craft as that of means to ends. 'Craft always involves a distinction between means and ends … strictly speaking it applies not to the things but to the actions concerned with them' (p 15). Importantly, Collingwood recognises that crafts consist in the actions involved in achieving the ends. The actions, of course, are skilful, not blind, and there is, I will take it straightway, an implicit acceptance that crafts consist in a kind of knowledge of how to bring about certain kinds of both physical and non-physical results. While the term 'craft' is used often to allude to the manipulation of physical means to produce artefacts, Collingwood recognises that not all crafts are directed towards producing artefacts; examples of craft discussed by him include horse breeding, the art of war, the writing of tragedies and comedies. In short, craft is the knowledge of how to 'bring human beings into certain states of body or mind conditions' (p 18).

This basic concept of bringing something about is understood by Collingwood in two senses of making: creation and fabrication. He says: 'Making an artefact, or acting according to craft thus consists of two sages: (1) making the plan, which is creation (2) imposing that plan on certain matter, which is fabricating' (p 133). In making this distinction, Collingwood characterises the concept of creation as non-technical: 'To create something means to make it non-technically, but yet consciously and voluntarily.' (p 128). In his view, technical expertise will be the province of the craftsman, but in so far as a person is an artist their creativity is distinct from any technical expertise they have. Collingwood's discussion of the activity of an engineer engaged in the project of building a bridge nicely illustrates his way of thinking about this distinction. The engineer will come up with a plan in his imagination and then execute it on materials to produce a physical work:

> When we speak of an engineer as making the plan, we are using the word 'make' in its other sense, as equivalent to create. Making a plan for a bridge is not imposing a certain form on certain matter, it is a making that is not a transforming, that is to say it is a creation. (p 133)

It is the creation of the *plan*, rather than the fabrication of the physical bridge for which it is the plan, that Collingwood terms analogous to the making of a work of art:

> When a man makes up a tune, he may and very often does at the same time hum it or sing it or play it on an instrument ... But all these are accessories of the real work ... the actual making of the tune is something that goes on in his head and nowhere else ... this is a case of creation, just as much as the making of a plan or a disturbance. Hence the making of a tune

is an instance of imaginative creation. The same applies to the making of a poem or a picture or any other work of art. (p 134)

Obviously, depending on the art selected for the comparison with the work of the engineer, the parallels may be drawn more or less closely. For example, a parallel with the sculptor will be a close one. Just like the engineer, the sculptor comes up with the idea for the work in his imagination and it will then be executed in physical materials. For the sculptor, too, it may take some time and organisation to pass from the phase of creation (which may of course occur while working on a model) to the stage of fabrication of the sculpture. In this vein, one is reminded of Alfred Hitchcock's claim that he visualised every film in his 'mind's eye' prior to its production; the production of the film, with the deployment of technical knowledge involved, he considered a secondary activity because the film had already been created in his imagination. Importantly, Collingwood does not disallow any activity from being genuinely artistic just because there is a stage of production or fabrication involving, usually, a large degree of technical knowledge. He accepts that there is a large degree of 'overlap' between craft and art, but the key mark of the distinction marking the border between the two stages is non-technical creation. A work is not considered art in virtue of the fabrication involved. If it is art, it will be art in virtue of the element of creation in its production. Collingwood describes this element, with regard to the example of Ben Jonson's poetry, as his 'imaginative vision' (p 20).

However, if close analogies may be drawn between the activity of artists and craftsmen, can one really persist in maintaining the distinction that Collingwood wishes to make? Collingwood says that creation is non-technical, but it is difficult to see in what significant sense this is supposed to be true. It is merely a truism to claim that a plan made by the engineer, though it regards technical matters, is not itself planned according to a technique and so, in that sense, may be described as non-technical. For the plan regards technical matters and its creation comprises technical knowledge. It is not merely that technical knowledge is a precondition for creating the plan for the bridge as, to take one of Collingwood's examples, certain conditions must be in place if one is to create a disturbance. That is to say, it is not the case that an act of creation occurs and the idea thus created is subsequently cast in technical terms in order to produce the work. Rather, to create a plan for a bridge is in itself the application of technical understanding; it is to bring to bear the technical knowledge which informs the actions directed to the production of the end. After all, a layman's sketch, by someone who is ignorant of engineering principles, does not constitute a plan for a bridge; in order to distinguish between an engineer's true plan for a bridge and a layman's napkin-sketch 'plan', appeal to the notion of specialised, technical knowledge possessed by the engineer is inescapable.

To create a poem is, in fact, to bring to bear one's technical knowledge of metre, alliteration, simile, rhyme and so forth to inform one's writing of the poem. The specific technical features present in the poem as a result of the deployment of general technical knowledge partly constitute the poem. Now Collingwood discusses the technical aspects of poetry when he tries to mark poetry off as art and not craft (p 20) because, he claims, it does not involve a means to an end. He draws an ironic comparison with the work of the blacksmith:

> lighting the forge, cutting a piece off a bar, heating it, and so on. What is analogous to these processes in the case of a poem? The poet may get paper and pen, fill the pen, sit down and square his elbows; but these actions are preparatory not to composition (which may go on in the poet's head) but to writing. Suppose the poem is a short one and composed without the use of writing materials; what are the means by which the poem composes it? I can think of no answer, unless comic answers are wanted, such as 'using a rhyming dictionary', 'pounding his foot on the floor or wagging his head or hand to mark the metre', or 'getting drunk'. If one looks at the matter seriously, one sees that the only factors in the situation are the poet, the poetic labour of his mind, and the poem. (p 20)

Collingwood's comparison with physical means is a red herring. Instead, the key point is that – while there may also be non-technical aspects to the poem – the fact that the creation of the poem occurs partly by means of technical knowledge shows that the claim that creation is essentially non-technical is false. In short, it seems that a purported exclusively non-technical notion of creation is not available to be employed in marking a distinction between art and craft. But if the presence or absence of technical knowledge is not the mark of the distinction between craft and 'art proper' is there a further basis for the distinction in Collingwood's book?

2. Craft and Preconceived Ideas

The notion of creation does not give us reason to draw a significant distinction between art and craft. However, there is a further part of Collingwood's analysis of craft that calls for discussion: the preconceived idea.

> It [craft] involves a distinction between planning and execution. The result to be obtained is preconceived or thought out before being arrived at; the craftsman knows what he wants to make before he makes it. This foreknowledge is absolutely indispensable to craft – moreover this foreknowledge is not vague, but precise. (pp 15-16)

For the kind of plan the engineer works to may be a request for a specific type of bridge just as a rider may request a specific type of horseshoe from the blacksmith. In such a case, the plan to which the engineer works will amount to a preconceived idea, and the artefact will be a 'ready to go' or 'off the rails' item, already worked out in advance of the request: a bridge copied from one location and transplanted to another, a standard type of horseshoe or style of portrait awaiting the commission of a renaissance patron. Indeed, this line of thinking chimes with an intuitive way of drawing a distinction between art and craft. For in so far as an engineer takes a bridge off the shelf, to coin a phrase, we would be tempted to say that he is merely a craftsman; by contrast, in so far as the engineer's brief allows him the freedom to invent – though clearly his technical knowledge comes into play – one is inclined to consider him creative and on a parallel with the artist. The contrast between Santiago Calatrava's *Samuel Beckett* and *James Joyce* bridges comes to mind.

Now, to draw out more clearly the import of what Collingwood is getting at here, return for a moment to our previous comparison of the engineer and the sculptor. Once each has created an
initial plan, each then knows what he wants to make and each
may then proceed to realise the plan by producing the material
work, the bridge or the sculpture. Insofar as each has created a
plan in his imagination, on Collingwood's terms each may be understood as artistic and for each of them the subsequent realisation of that plan is mere craft. So, simply knowing in advance of
realisation what artefact one intends to realise cannot be what
Collingwood means by preconceived idea, because it will not
mark out the capacity to deploy one's technical knowledge creatively: it will blur the distinction between creatively deploying
one's technical knowledge and utilising technical knowledge to
fabricate an 'off the rail' item. It behoves us to construe Collingwood's point, I think, as follows: the engineer or artist armed with
a preconceived idea does not create, either in a technical or non-
technical sense: his foreknowledge allows him to bypass the stage
of creation altogether and move right to realisation of the artefact.
Intuitively, when a preconceived idea is being implemented, it is
one of the clearest cases that we would not count as artistic activity.
Examples where one person creates and others implement: ses-
sion musicians, the renaissance apprentice in the great artist's
workshop and so on. In these cases, these seem clear examples
which merit the description 'craftsmen but not artists' and the
guiding idea here is the notion of preconception.

Now while craftsmen may in many cases merely implement
preconceived ideas, this is not necessarily the case. The problem
with Collingwood's notion of craft as marked by the preconceived idea is that it assumes that craft is a static activity in which
means and ends, plans and standard means of execution are given
for once and for all. However, craft is often a dynamic activity and
developing the craft requires imagination – one might say 'imaginative vision' – and innovation in a given medium. An example of
art 'falsely so called' developed in a new way is Shakespeare's
Othello, in which going against the standard rules of tragedy, the
crisis occurs very early in the second act. Merely in terms of the

technicalities of plot, that is, it stands out in relation to Shakespeare's other tragedies. Of course, one may be tempted to say that the implication of Collingwood's view is that the artist is the 'ideas' man while the craftsman is an artisan who technically implements that idea, and Shakespeare incorporated both roles in one man. More recently, this notion of the artist as distinct from the craftsman in virtue of being an 'ideas man' is endorsed by Arthur Danto in his book *Andy Warhol*:

> The artist had the ideas: there was no reason why he had to make the material objects that embodied those ideas ... In any case, it is no longer part of the concept of original art that it actually be made by the artist who takes credit for it. It was enough that he conceived the idea that it exemplified. (pp 54-55)

But the notion of craft as a dynamic enterprise suggests that the notion of the 'ideas man' is not at all as straightforward as it seems. Contrasted with the dynamic aspect of craft, the artist will be an 'ideas man' not in a sense that he is imaginative, innovative or original while the craftsman is not, but in the sense that he is a man who we might be tempted to say deals in the 'right' sort of ideas; one might well begin to doubt that there are going to be 'right' or appropriate sorts of ideas for art to the exclusion of craft.

3. Craft and Appreciation

It is a simple point that understanding the craft involved in production of a work enriches appreciation of it in ways that go beyond just recognising it as an exercise in craft; one is not merely admiring the technical virtuosity involved and then switching back to appreciating the work 'as-a-work-of-art'. Take, as it happens, the example of an artist favoured by Collingwood, the mature Cézanne, and a work such as *Mountains in Provence*. Knowing that Cézanne is prioritising form and colour to convey the sharp edges of rocks in the foreground, and only minimally using perspective, counts in favour of appreciating the painting largely in tactile terms rather than as essentially a visual experience, and counts against considering it as an early critic of Cézanne's commented, the product of 'a diseased retina' (reported

in *The Life and Work of Cézanne* by Edmund Swinglehurst, p 37).
Understanding the particular ways in which a work has been
crafted may often be of benefit for appreciating it in ways beyond
those particular respects in which it has been crafted. This contribution made by a grasp of craft in enabling appreciation of a particular work in respects beyond the technicalities of its crafted respects counts strongly, I suggest, in favour of the significance of
craft to art.

   Appreciation of a work is notably enriched by understanding
it as part of a developing tradition and craft has proved itself a
powerful rationale of development in the history of art. In light of
the achievement of the Italian renaissance, for example, in estab-
lishing the rules of linear perspective the innovation of many subsequent movements in the history of art, such as Impressionism
and after that Cubism were moves away from perspective, and
the realism associated with it, as the key to visual representation.
Ernst Gombrich, for example, expresses how an issue of craft may
drive such general dynamism in the following way:

> The Cubists continued where Cézanne had left off. Hence-
> forward an increasing number of artists took it for granted that
> what matters in art is to find new solutions for what are called
> problems of 'form'. To these artists, then, 'form' always comes
> first and the 'subject' second.' (*The Story of Art*, p 448)

In turn, following the innovations of Cubism, Marcel
Duchamp's innovations, in works such as *The Bride Stripped Bare
by Bachelors, Even* were an attempt to move more sharply again
away from what he referred to as 'the retinal' in favour of the conceptual. A similar case may also be made for expression in art.

   To advance the objection that this is merely appreciation of the
means of representation, or the *means* of expression, would be to
make a mistake that is implicit in Collingwood's view: the mistake that one can separate interest in that which gets represented
from the way in which it is represented, or interest in that which
gets expressed from the way in which it is expressed. That is the
idea that one could label one interest in the 'art proper' ingredient
and the other interest in the 'craft' ingredient. The mistake is palpable

when one realises that after such a separation one would be left with the simple interest in the object represented, or the emotion expressed – and this fails to account for why, in matters of art, the point is to divert interest to artworks rather than stimulate interest directly in the objects they represent or the emotions they express. Appreciation of the means of representation or indeed expression is inextricably blended with interest in the represented or the expressed, and knowledge of craft ultimately enables a more thorough appreciation of these means for both the creator of art and the audience and that is powerful reason to consider that the concept of craft is crucial to art.

4. Concluding Comments

The suggestion that art (understood in Collingwood's terms of a process of self-clarification of emotion) is peculiarly suited to offer consolation by helping one to address fundamental concerns in a personal crisis, has run into some difficulty. Collingwood fails to establish his case against craft, and considering his failure together with positive reasons outlined for considering craft to be crucial to art, the conclusion is that one does not in fact have reason to think that art is peculiarly suited to the vehicle of self-clarification of emotion relevant to consolation. More broadly, though, with regard to the question of whether philosophy in general provides consolation in a personal crisis, perhaps occasioned by an economic one, the moral of the story is as follows. By emphasising the 'philosophy of –', the suggestion is that philosophy, to borrow a term from Plato, has a 'guardian' role. That is, philosophy does not offer ready consolation in terms of being a direct guide to practical, substantive steps or decisions about one's affairs in a crisis but rather to provide skills that, indirectly, assist in weighing up proposed consolations. To draw an analogy between the attempt to recover from a personal crisis and attempts to recover from an economic one, the study of philosophy constitutes a 'personal climate' along the lines of an 'investment climate'. The study of philosophy may be compared to taxes and interest rates – they will not make you start a business, they will not tell you what kind of business to start or how to run it, they will not make your debtors pay on time or at all, and many other factors are required for your business to be a success, but they will strongly influence whatever business you do start.

Bibiography of works in which the topic of craft receives discussion to greater and lesser extents:

Aristotle, *Poetics*, trs and ed James Hutton, London and New York, W. W. Norton & Company 1982

Collingwood, R. G., *The Principles of Art*, Oxford, OUP 1958 (Clarendon Press 1938)

Danto, Arthur C., *Andy Warhol*, New Haven and London, Yale University Press 2009

Dewey, John, *Art as Experience*, New York, Perigree 2005 (Penguin 1934)

Plato, *The Republic*, trs Desmond Lee, London, Penguin, 1987

Scruton, Roger, *The Aesthetics of Architecture*, Princeton, Princeton University Press 1979

Swinglehurst, Edmund, *The Life and Works of Cézanne*, Paragon, 1994.

CHAPTER TEN

Against Philosophical Consolation

Paal Antonsen

Once during a dinner conversation, Gore Vidal asked Noël Coward 'Is it true that you've never had sex with a woman?' Coward could affirm this, but an unconvinced Vidal continued 'not even with Gertrude Lawrence?' – to which Coward responded resolutely, 'particularly not, Miss Lawrence'. Standing in opposition to the other essays in this collection, this one attempts to convince you that academic subjects are not in the business of providing consolation, should neither pretend nor present themselves as they are, and that philosophy is particularly not.

One may ask initially, how could philosophy bring about consolation? Unlike some other endeavours philosophy does not aim to heal the sick, make the streets safe at night, feed the poor or repair elevators. Some aims overlap, so by achieving your original goal you have at the same time achieved another. If you aim at helping people in distress or alleviating poverty, you also to a large extent do provide consolation in the same process. Then, what is the aim of philosophy? Many would subscribe to the slogan that aiming at truth is the main thing, but in all fairness, it is the only thing. In this respect, it is not all too different from other academic disciplines. What makes it particular is its generality and abstractness.

The two propositions I submit for you to consider are as follows: firstly, that philosophy does not bring consolation in any important sense, and secondly, that philosophy should not aim at bringing consolation. Both these propositions are tightly connected with the idea that philosophy first and foremost aims at truth. If philosophy happens to console a handful of individuals (for reasons that completely escape me), then that is purely coincidental and does not take away the general point. Those who claim that philosophy does or ought to have as its aim bringing about consolation places on it a heavier burden than it can possibly be expected to bear, and in the process ruins what made philosophy worthwhile in the first place.

1

With the question settled, and the answer gestured towards, we need to add the context in which it is meant to arise. Imagine a second-hand and peripheral part of an expanding and possibly imploding universe; in a solar system where there's almost no life; in a collection of mercilessly evolving eco-systems where we were never meant to be; and where the most curious of all plots unfolded. A small group of apes began to think that everything had to be about 'them' – that is 'us'. Some took that thought even further, going from the plural to the singular. They came to think that everything was really about 'me'. This plot has resulted in the near, and likely inevitable, destruction of the planetary eco-systems, a recurrent state of financial crises, reduction of collective welfare and solidarity, and where the smallest geographical distance can determine whether one will be born in luxury or poverty. On this planet, sympathy is often measured in miles. Imagine this and you have imagined our context.

One should have divined the coming of the current financial crisis, if for nothing else, because of the rise in sales enjoyed by the wooden pen of Ayn Rand. One has to admit, if only from a curious observer's point of view, that there is something strangely fascinating as well as puzzling about such people; those who after having contemplated the current state of our planet, including the monetary imbalance and social injustice, make the remarkable entailment and conclusion that what must be wrong with this world is that people just haven't been selfish enough. 'Ethics is salve for the poor' is the slogan invoked by such a thought. Despite such tendencies – or if 'tendencies' is too nice a word 'calamities' will do – despite these, time is long past for the all too blatant realisation that monetary gain may be the aim of Mammon, but not so for Man, and that we should be erecting no new temples for either. In short, it should have been brought home to us that private vices do not yield public virtues.

It is not uncommon that when the conditions of a society are in decline, the escapist ideologies are on the rise. It is understandable that if a society's material conditions fail to provide proper living standards or when the gap between public opinion and public policy becomes too wide, one turns to fantasies to take one's mind away from these issues. The clearest example of such fantasies is religion, but also philosophy as in the morals of the Roman Stoics, who advise us to simply reconcile ourselves with nature's determinism – be you slave or sufferer – or the Platonic and Christian traditions with their alluring tales of a more genuine and real world in another dimension. Priests and philosophers, when either asked to or exploiting the opportunity, aim at showing how, since this world is in such a dismal state, one can get out of this place. This is the impulse I want us to reject.

There are two familiar ideas of how philosophy is a consoling force within the current context: either by directing philosophy inwards as an individual comforter, or by directing philosophy outward, giving a promise of something beyond the misery. What they both share is the familiar scent of narcissism. The idea is that not only are humans the most interesting part of the world for humans, but that the world as a whole must share this view. Furthermore, theories about the world are subservient to our desires. It's not my intention to build a straw man, so I bought one instead. Alain de Botton, in his book *The Consolations of Philosophy*,[1] writes in the spirit of Epicurus's proclamation:

> Any philosopher's argument which does not therapeutically treat human suffering is worthless, for just as there is no profit in medicine when it does not expel the diseases of the body, so there is no profit in philosophy when it does not expel the diseases of the mind.

Just as we turn to physicians when our bodies are unwell, de Botton informs us, so 'we should turn to philosophers for the same reason when our soul is unwell'. Apart from the fact that the soul actually is the body, the analogy would be better expressed as 'just as some turn to homeopathy when their bodies are un-

1. de Botton, A. (2001) *The Consolations of Philosopy*, Penguin, London

well, so some turn to philosophy when their soul is unwell.' At least these two share the same amount (or lack) of empirical evidence to serve those functions. About the normative issue, consider this at first: if philosophy's success were measured and geared toward curing us of our melancholy and private misfortunes, a text book in the history of philosophy would be thinner than the bible became after Thomas Jefferson took out his razorblade. Philosophy, as all like-minded endeavours, ought to flow from the inherent curiosity of people and not some external demand. Also, for every three philosophers you meet you will have twenty different suggestions for a cure. Chances are you'll be washing down your tears with poison. The only reason I can think of why anyone would follow a philosopher anywhere would have to be out of pure curiosity. As a conjurer's trick, de Botton and those who sympathise with him are attempting to assure us that not only is it surprisingly simple to achieve consolation in the face of one's existential dilemmas, but also that a surprisingly simple philosophy will do this for you.

The second kind is more an impulse or a sentiment. It is the same one that gives rise to varieties of Platonism and religious doctrine. The main idea is that philosophy can open a door to a world outside of this one. Now that the coffers are empty, and not only its inhabitants but the planet itself is running out of luck, we can dream up a new one where mistakes are corrected and morality restored – all without doing the hard work of achieving this for the world we happen to live in. The truth, however, is far less glamorous. A poignant, if sobering reply, is that philosophy often consists in spending hours, indeed years, on thinking about problems that won't go away, on subjects that don't matter, for people who don't care – and why should they? I no more demand of other people that they should care and share my interest in formal semantics any more than I demand this about strategy games, for which I have also acquired a taste. It is not sufficient to think about changing the world. In fact it often takes away the focus of doing something. Merely philosophising about it will be as helpful as all the chemical knowledge in the world is for someone caught on a sinking ship.

I know that I am in effect telling you 'philosophers can't be of much use', but it is not as masochistic as it sounds. Philosophy has its use and its place, but this must not be mistaken for a subordinate service to our mental health or as a guide to a better world existing beyond. In a universe that doesn't care about you, don't think philosophy has more of a heart.

2

Let us turn to the first main claim, that philosophy does not bring you consolation. The progress achieved in philosophy, when at its most successful, has been the development of more sophisticated formal methods and taking down prevailing dogmas – in particular by taking us away from mysticism and religion into an appreciation of the human condition as one of the many branches priding the evolutionary tree. Philosophy has fortunately been dethroned from the title given by Kant as 'the Queen of the sciences'. Legends apart, it does not provide any kind of special or different truth from other academic subjects; it is simply one of the many ways we attempt to unweave the rainbow. A more fitting title for the subject in a democratic age would be the Roman title 'first among equals'.

The first reason why philosophy does not provide consolation is the independent nature of truth. The distinction between a true belief and a desirable belief would be blurred if aiming at truth were to coincide with aiming to please. Whether or not you want it to be the case, the sentence 'Napoleon invaded Russia in 1812' is true. No degree of wishful thinking is going to change that. The mind cannot change matter, at least not matters such as history, physics and philosophy. Truth applies to all kinds of sentences, and philosophers happen to be mostly concerned with ones such as 'do proper names refer?', 'could there have been other things than there are?', 'is knowledge the same as a justified true belief?' There is nothing exceptional about these sentences separating the ones philosophers use from the ones that non-philosophers use. They are made up of the same symbols and syntax as the ones you use in everyday life. Philosophers just tend to put them together to express abstract thoughts and go about somewhat more rigorously when attempting to assess their truth-value.

But it is important that one does not confuse truth with certainty. Just because there is a truth of the matter whether or not unicorns could have existed, that does not mean one gains certainty in the proposed answers. The task of aiming at truth is not the 'absolute' notion of truth that many cultural critics balk at. With Platonism's and Theism's fall from grace, the consequence is not, as many public intellectuals will have you believe, that the wicked is elevated and the good devalued; the wrong held high and the right held low. Truth isn't true for you or true for me. Truth isn't true for anyone or anything. It is too much of an independent mind for that. Furthermore, what makes a sentence true is completely independent of what would console our angst or get us through the night. This, however, does not mean that truth has any glamorous or absolute character. It is simply a property certain sentences happen to have, a property philosophers happen to be concerned about. Neither does it mean that you can't take pleasure from certain sentences being true. For example, I find it a happy state of affairs that the sentence 'there are no gods' is true. What it does mean is that the relation is a coincidental one.

This attitude gives us a certain conception of the world. Recall this famous sceptical scenario: imagine the possibility that you might just be a brain-in-a-vat, and that all your apparent knowledge is provided by tiny wires that send feed-back into your brain. You are cut off from the world, but for these small wires that pulsate into the cortex. A disturbing fantasy, to be sure, but let's not get our hopes up: we are brains in a vat – fleshy, slimy, short-lived ones at that, with nothing but surface irritations on our nerve-endings to prevent us from being caught in epistemic and emotional isolation. These irritations, transmitted up the spinal cord into the vertebrate canal and firing of neurons at simultaneous places in our brain, a place riddled with junk genes and parasites, with no respect or regard for phenomenology, constitute the fundamental level of our human condition. The brain as a series of processes, executed in an algorithmic environment that is genetically determined, is as good as it gets. Fortunately for us, it is also as good as it needs to be. Philosophy, or any other activity that is exercised by our cognitive abilities has emerged from this background pandemonium. It helps to clarify our thoughts if we remind ourselves about this, for any philosophy worth its salt is one that holds hands with science. It is the realm of nature that is the realm of philosophy. It may not be pretty, it may consist mostly of things that will kill you and make you into food for worms, and it may be a floating orb of magma and maggots – but it's home.

Seeing ourselves in the wake of Darwin as creatures who come up with trickier ways to deal with their environment, as bundles of molecules avoiding other bundles of molecules in a more and more elegant dance, takes away the idea that there is something in the world (humans apart) that could provide us with purpose and meaning. This is not to defend a view sometimes called 'naturalism' by its defenders and 'scientism' by its deniers. It is simply the recognition that one must accept as true the sentences we for the moment have most evidence for. However, bring those two ideas together: the independence of truth and our Darwinian past. If our grasp of truth has emerged from the evolutionary background, then it must have done so in the same manner as justification – what constitutes warrant for making assertions. As our way of knowing is interpretations of our environments, the only route we have to truth is the same route as justification. Aiming at truth does coincide with something, namely aiming at finding justification and evidence for our sentences. So much the worse for those who claim to have knowledge beyond our collective scientific efforts. We move onwards as a matter of persuading each other of the inherent merits of our ideas according to their compatibility with our initial bumping into other objects. Those who claim to have knowledge of a world beyond this one by faith or rhetoric ignore the common source of truth and justification. Providing none of the latter, they fail to provide any of the former. Apes like us can only come to know what apes like us are able to grasp. Truth gains its role in the natural world by our semantic ascent – going from the fact that pigs are pink to evaluating the truth of the sentence 'pigs are pink'. Semantic considerations came into our view when we moved from being mere vehicles of our genes to being vehicles that can talk about what it's like being vehicles of our genes. That kind of talk might give rise to the desire of consolation, and also the desire to console, but again this has little to do with philosophy.

Philosophy attempts to develop theories about the world, but human happiness has no clear place in the design of the universe. No one guaranteed us anything, no one promised us anything. We are left to our own devices and should not lament our misfortunes, for there is no place to direct the blame. Perhaps we do sometimes feel the *Weltschmerz*, perhaps the meaninglessness of the dark eyes of the moon cause distress, and perhaps you spend your nights wishing you were somewhere else or indeed someone else. Such is our meagre lot in this life. As a human I could feel for you, as a philosopher I could do much, much less. If you want philosophy to tell you differently, you change its realm from fact to fiction. Philosophy may be concerned with the nature of the mental state you are in when you are depressed, but it doesn't concern itself with the fact that you are depressed. That our lives did not turn out the way they ought to have done is a fault of design one may say, but philosophy works on the laws, not the flaws, of nature.

Seeing philosophy as an integral part of the study of the natural world has taken us over to the second reason why philosophy does not provide consolation: there is nothing philosophy tells you about the world that makes it into a place desirable to be – there is no consolation to be gained from truth. It is in this respect the most boring property a sentence can hope to achieve. We are twice removed cousins of the chimpanzees, with an extraordinary long history of extraordinary suffering, where our genes couldn't care less about us, and if you pray to the sky above the best you can hope for is that it doesn't rain on you. No amount of wishing and believing can change this. Furthermore, philosophy's concern with technical questions of scope of quantification, vague predicates and the analysis of counterfactuals won't bring that skip back in your jump or that twinkle in your eye. It is only our capacity for solidarity that gives purpose and consolation in this world. We should leave philosophy to talk about the world as it and act as we want it to be.

3

The fact that philosophy does not in its current state provide consolation (or when it does it is false consolation) does not preclude that it *should* perform this task. The Epicurean proclamation could still be correct, in which case most philosophy ever done has been a waste of time. That is perfectly possible either way, of course. There are two main reasons I want to voice as to why philosophy shouldn't pursue the task of consoling. The first is disciplinary, which relates to the initial aim of philosophy, whereas the second is personal, in the sense that the demand for it is symptomatic of narcissism.

The first point is very simple: if you change the aim, you change the discipline. If the aim of philosophy where changed from aiming at truth to aiming to please, it would no longer be what we know as philosophy. Philosophy would be at odds with what it, together with the other sciences, has taught us about the world. The suggestion that philosophy should shift its aim is similar to Voltaire's polemic suggestion that religion may not be right, but it's something the peasants should believe. It would be the best way to ensure that second-rate thinking became the main order of the day.

Imagine what it would be like if philosophy were to aim at consolation. We often take consolation from what we already know or that which we are familiar with. The philosopher would then be asked to defend the *status quo*. But the problem is that the *status quo* is not, as it were, philosophy's *status quo* – philosophy thrives in the face of received opinion. Quite the opposite of supporting our self-image, the best philosophy is drawn out from conflict and with a certain combative yet ironic stance. A term more fitting the role of a philosopher would be 'radical', for those who could make themselves deserve such a noble term, but also more maligned ones like 'rebel', 'contrarian', 'maverick', 'the devil's brood' or any term that opposes ruling ideas would do. A philosopher should side with Milton's Lucifer any day, as only in resistance to authority will imagination blossom. There was a saying in ancient Rome: 'Do justice and let the skies fall'. That would go for philosophy as well. Let the facts be whatever they happen to be. Let the chips fall as the may. Any attempt to tame philosophy by a narcissistic demand is to turn away from the task of understanding the world to the best of our abilities, to the task of focusing on the worst in us. Philosophy should seek out the comforting, consoling cushions of our minds and rather measure its success by the count of the kill. A useful philosophy is one that together with the methods of science and the ironies of poetry, disrupts the *status quo* and takes us to a society as far away from this one as ours is to the ancient Assyrian.

Turning to the more personal, one might think that philosophical consolation lies not in the familiar, but in the individual. The pleasures achieved by a contemplative mind are reflected in the idea of the philosopher as an introvert soul-searcher, a solitary monk or an armchair dilettante. After all, in the *Nicomachean Ethics*, Aristotle assures us that the happiest life is one aimed at contemplation. Despite the somewhat romantic overtones of this picture, we should not fail to see its unpleasant undertones. If Aristotle's happy man was someone we should hold as a paragon example, philosophy would turn into another route of escapism. The demand for consolation may ask us to tend to our souls, but there is no point in watering a garden where nothing can bloom anyway. The body has no soul, so there is nothing to attend to, unless the idea only means that one should attend to one's own or other consenting individuals' bodies. That has its redeeming factors and even its rewards, but it has little to do with the task of honest inquiry. We must abandon the idea that the good life is the one that has withdrawn itself from its obligations to others. We should especially be suspicious of any idea that consolation is found in the avoidance of conflict, either with our own or other people's ideas. Rather, we should be in continuous conflict with our comrades, and seek a life with and out, but not without, scepticism and doubt. Good philosophy seeks not consolation but confrontation.

4

Up until now I have been running the risk of sounding a bit too bleak. It is not my intention to maintain that there is no consolation to be found inside this world, only that it is outside of philosophy. As an alternative, I submit that to in order to achieve genuine consolation we must abandon the private and turn to the public. Consolation is to be found in fighting against the plot of the apes I mentioned in the initial scenario. It was this selfishness and narcissism that caused the problems that made us desire consolation in the first place. The answer can surely not be to continue this line by asking for a more narcissistic philosophy. Let us not remove the symptoms but the cause of the disease.

It is a sign of a relatively free and wealthy society that its inhabitants have the opportunity to pursue philosophy. It is therefore an oddity that we, as members of such a society, are not only calling out for consolation but do so from an activity that already makes us privileged. We make mockery of ourselves by desiring philosophical consolation, in thinking that we are in some special need for sympathy and concern. In the mentioned context of ecological, financial and humanitarian crises, philosophy cannot do much for those who are really suffering. The consolation to be gained for oneself must be provided through consoling others.

The current industrial civilisation has sprung forth riding on the back of certain unhelpful philosophical ideas. The crucial and core idea is that the individual ought to seek material gain, and when he has reached some stable level of income and possession, there is no end to the line of existential problems promoted by media and academic charlatans.[2] It takes little reflection to understand that as long as this philosophical idea is allowed to play a prominent role in our collective consciousness, the world will be destroyed in a relatively small amount of time. A society built on material gain and narcissism is a suicidal one, and its own doom is within our view. The financial crisis could be a call, but it would be a wrong move to think that philosophy would be the place to take shelter. What we are obligated to do is to give shelter to those more unfortunate than us in the community as a whole – and by that we should mean the global community. The real need for consolation is far too serious to be left to philosophy.

2. For a case that some philosophers intentionally deceive their audience, see Bricmont & Sokal (1998) *Intellectual Impostures*, Profile Books, London

The cure of the narcissistic view may lie in the adoption of a more ironic and democratic sentiment. My thought is perfectly exemplified by Wilfred Owen's *A Terre*, replying to Shelley's romanticised nature.

> Certainly flowers have the easiest time on earth.
> 'I shall be one with nature, herb, and stone.'
> Shelley would tell me. Shelley would be stunned;
> The dullest Tommy hugs that fancy now.
> 'Pushing up daisies,' is their creed, you know.

Written in the trenches of the Great War, Owen brings the elevated poetry of Shelley down to earth where we are moulded with mud and blood. The ironic sentiment should give us inspiration not to attend to our immaterial soul while the material soil for future generations is laid waste. We express our most intimate thoughts and deepest love by flowers – the very flowers that are nourished by the rotting carcasses of our predecessors. This thought should bring a wintery smile on anyone's face. The common fate and shared future awaiting us all is manure. It is by accepting this with an ironic attitude and not by denial or philosophical distraction that we gain consolation in the face of the slow but very noticeable decline of our bodies. Owen reminds us that we shouldn't be looking after, and in some cases forward to, our afterlives, but we should be looking after, and in all cases forward to, the lives after ours.

It has been thought that philosophers are all too eager to grasp any chance they have to play a prominent role – such as telling you how you should live. Don't believe everything you hear about philosophers, but don't disbelieve it either. It's true that nobody wants to be leaders, other than the people you don't want to have as leaders. Therefore, mistrust the siren call of philosophers who claim to hold the key to happiness. Philosophers are as lost and misguided as the rest. There is no empirical evidence that supports the idea that philosophers lead any happier or more ethical lives than say art historians or pastry chefs. The philosophers who are peacocking and pretending to guard the deep truths unattainable by the masses are mere 'sphinxes without secrets'.

List of Contributors

Paal Antonsen is a PhD student in philosophy at Trinity College Dublin. Prior to moving to Ireland, he did a BA and MA in philosophy at the University of Bergen, Norway. His areas of specialisation are aesthetics, philosophy of language and logic.

Dónall Mc Ginley did a BA in mediaeval and modern Irish at NUI Maynooth, before doing a BA in philosophy at King's College London and an MA in mediaeval studies at University College Dublin. He is currently doing a PhD at Trinity College Dublin on the metaphysics of the 14th century Scottish philosopher John Duns Scotus.

Ciarán McGlynn has lectured on many areas of philosophy, in particular on ancient and medieval philosophy, pragmatism, and the philosophy of religion. His current research interests are on Edmund Burke and Enlightenment thought.

Joseph McLoughlin is a graduate of Trinity College Dublin. Following a spell at King's College London, he carried out postgraduate research on Freud at Trinity, which has led to an ongoing interest in the study of irrationality. Philosophical interests also include aesthetics and Scottish commonsense philosophy. He has been involved in the study and teaching of philosophy for a number of years.

Gwen Murphy is a graduate of Trinity College, Dublin, where she read philosophy and is now a postgraduate. Her dissertation focuses on the relationship between virtue and education, and virtue and knowledge, in Plato, with a view to gaining new insights into contemporary educational thinking. She is also a trained Montessori teacher.

Brendan O'Byrne studied in Trinity College Dublin and wrote his doctoral thesis on Plato. His specialisation is ancient philosophy and he also has a strong interest in phenomenology, ethics, and philosophy of technology. He is the Curator of the Plato Centre, a cross-institutional research facility based in TCD.

Paul O'Grady is a lecturer and Fellow of Trinity College Dublin, having previously taught at Oxford University. His research deals with theory of knowledge and philosophy of religion. He has published *Relativism* (2002), *Philosophical Theology* (2008) as well as numerous articles and chapters on these issues and is also a qualified psychotherapist.

Peter Simons FBA studied mathematics and philosophy at Manchester. He held positions at Bolton, Salzburg and Leeds, before becoming Chair of Moral Philosophy at Trinity College Dublin in 2009. His main areas of research are metaphysics and its applications, and the history of 19th and 20th century philosophy in Central Europe.

Manfred Weltecke studied philosophy and biology in Bonn and Dublin. After his first Staatsexamen he worked as a self-employed technical translator, writer and editor. In 2004 he enrolled as a graduate student in the philosophy department of Trinity College. He received his PhD in 2009 for a dissertation on Kant's theory of knowledge. He is married to graphic-designer Martine Maguire-Weltecke. They have three children.

Glossary

A Posteriori: A belief is epistemologically justified in an *a posteriori* manner if its justification relies on experience.

A Priori: A belief is epistemologically justified in an *a priori* manner if its justification does not rely on experience.

Aesthetics: The branch of philosophy which deals with art and beauty.

Agnosticism: An epistemological position about an area which denies that we are in a position to know about that area. In philosophy of religion this applies specifically to questions about God.

Analytical Philosophy: A tradition in contemporary philosophy mainly associated with the English-speaking world which privileges logical analysis, clarity and rigour.

Antinomies: Paradoxes.

Appearance: Used in the appearance/reality distinction. How things seem to be, which may not be actually how they are.

Argument: A set of propositions which are structured as premises to a conclusion. The premises operate as reasons which lead to the conclusion. This abstract conception of an argument needs to be distinguished from the more normal conception of an argument as a heated debate between opponents. The former conception is the normal one in philosophy.

Assumption: Another word for a premiss, or something which is assumed in an argument. It might be claimed to be obvious, or else is the conclusion of an earlier argument

Atomism: The metaphysical position which holds that the fundamental constituents of reality are small, indivisible, physical units, called atoms.

Belief: A mental state in which one holds something to be true. Note that a belief in this sense can be about anything, it is not restricted to being a religious notion.

Categories: The most general classifications, the basic kinds of features of things, for example quantity and quality.

Causation: A fundamental feature of the world is the pervasiveness of events causing other events. The analysis of causation is the attempt to explain the general features of this phenomenon, for example are there causal powers in things, or is causation a projection from our minds?

Cognition: How beings acquire knowledge of themselves and their environment.

Consciousness: The peculiar phenomenon of having a point of view, having a perspective, which is at the basis of subjectivity. There may be levels of consciousness and kinds of consciousness. It remains very hard to explain in objective terms.

Copernican Revolution: Originally referring to Nicholas Copernicus's astronomical theories which stated that the earth was not the centre of the cosmos, but rather rotated about the sun. It is sometimes also used to refer to Kant's epistemological theories which emphasised the constructive role of the mind.

Cosmological Argument: A kind of argument for the existence of God which argues from some observable feature of the cosmos to God as the best explanation of that feature.

Cosmos: The entire universe, considered as an ordered whole.

Deism: The view that there is a God who is responsible for the order evident in the universe, but who doesn't have ongoing contact with that universe and who is not an appropriate object of religious worship.

Deity: A term used to refer to God. For monotheists there can only be one deity, whereas polytheists hold there are many deities.

Determinism: The position which holds that everything which occurs is predetermined by antecedant causes, thereby denying genuine free-will.

Dialectic: Another term for philosophical argumentation.

Dilemma: An argument in which a position is shown to lead to two results, neither of which are acceptable. These results are known as the horns of the dilemma.

Dogmatism: The position which holds firmly to a view in the absence of any supporting argumentation, or without adequately dealing with opposed views.

Dualism: In philosophy of mind, the position that holds that mind and body are genuinely distinct substances.

Eliminativism: In philosophy of mind, the position that holds that mind does not genuinely exist, it can be eliminated as a useful term and replaced with a scientific account of brain states.

Emergentism: In philosophy of mind, the position that holds that mind is a by-product of body, a function that emerges as bodies become more complex.

Empiricism: The epistemological position which claims that knowledge ultimately derives from the senses and which tends to be suspicious of putative non-sensory knowledge (e.g. metaphysical knowledge).

Enlightenment: A period in intellectual history in Europe in the 18th century in which reason was idealised and superstition shunned.

Epistemology: The part of philosophy which examines knowledge, its nature, kinds, sources and causes.

Essence: The feature of things which explains what kind of thing it is, what gives it its identity.

Ethics: The part of philosophy which examines practical reasoning, specifically about the good, justice, rights, duty, virtue and obligations.

Existence: The feature of things which explains their instantiation, that they are actually there at all.

Existentialism: A school of philosophy whose origins are in the 19th century and which flourished in 20th century continental Europe. It emphasised themes such as authenticity, meaninglessness, freedom of choice and absurdity. Associated with Kierkegaard, Nietzsche, Sartre, Heidegger, Marcel.

Externalism: An epistemological doctrine which holds that in order to know something, it is not necessary to know that you know, i.e. one can know something without being able to rationally defend one's claim to knowledge of that thing.

Fideism: A position in philosophy of religion which holds that reason cannot affect faith, they are two separate and non-connected realms. Faith may well contradict reason, but this is acceptable, as they are separate. Associated with Kierkegaard and Kant.

Form: In Aristotle's metaphysics this refers to the structure which gives anything its identity. For Plato it refers to an abstract entity, beyond space and time, which is the reference of general terms, such as 'goodness'.

Formal Logic: The branch of logic which systematises arguments and uses symbolism to do so.

Free Will: The view that our actions are not predetermined by antecedent causes, whether physical or theological

Genetic Fallacy: An informal logical error in which causes for a belief are confused with reasons for the belief. For example, arguing that since someone believes in the existence of God on the basis of indoctrination (a cause), therefore there aren't good reasons for believing in God, is fallacious. Despite dubious causal origins, the belief may still be true.

Gettier Problem: A challenge to the traditional definition of knowledge as 'justified true belief'. Edmund L. Gettier devised counter-examples to this, in which all three of these conditions were fulfilled, yet our intuitions tend to deny that knowledge really exists in the example. Hence knowledge requires a fourth condition.

Hellenistic: Adjective pertaining to later Greek philosophy, after the death of Aristotle (322 BCE)

Idealism: A metaphysical position which holds that mind is fundamental to the basic nature of reality. Opposed to Realism. Idealism comes in various forms.

Identity: What something is, in its most general sense. Metaphysics seeks to articulate grounds for identity and to establish how identity relates to change, e.g. what sorts of changes make something change its identity?

Identity Theory: In philosophy of mind the materialist position that the mind and brain are identical.

Inference: In logic, the moving from one proposition to another in a rational way.

Infinite Regress: A chain of causes or reasons which has no beginning and which stretches to infinity.

Informal Logic: The logic of ordinary language, contrasted with formal logic. Involves the presentation of forms of argument and how arguments go wrong, i.e. fallacies.

Innate: Usually associated with ideas. Ideas are innate if they are inborn, not coming from outside.

Intentionality: The feature of mental states (such as ideas) that they are 'about' something.

Justice: The principled operation of equality or fairness in a person and society. It covers issues such as the distribution of benefits and burdens (distributive justice) and how to deal with injustice (retributive justice).

Justification: In epistemology, justification is the process by which one gives reasons for holding a belief to be true.

Karma: A Hindu and Buddhist doctrine which postulates a cosmic system of cause and effect and which specifically claims that actions have consequences which may well stretch beyond the bounds of this life.

Knowledge: The object of epistemology. Traditionally defined as 'justified true belief'.

Linguistic Turn: A feature of 20th century philosophy, where many of the traditional problems of philosophy are tackled by focusing on the use of language associated with them.

Logic: The science of inference – moving validly from one proposition to another with the goal of preserving truth. Formal logic is an abstract symbolic analysis of this process, informal logic is its use in normal discourse.

Logical Positivism: The empiricist movement associated with the Vienna Circle in the 1920s which attacked metaphysical doctrines and advocated a scientific style of philosophy.

Materialism: The metaphysical position which holds that the realm nature of reality is material, thereby denying the existence of mind or spirit.

Matter: In Aristotle's metaphysics, that which underlies form.

Metaphysics: The branch of philosophy which deals with the fundamental nature of reality

Modernity: A term used to describe the intellectual climate of the modern world, often in explicit contrast to classical or medieval ideas.

Modus Ponens: A common form of inference of the type 'If P then Q, P, therefore Q'. For example 'If it rains then the ground is wet', 'It is raining', therefore 'The ground is wet'.

Monotheism: Taken as synonymous with theism – that there is one, eternal and perfect creator God.

Natural Theology: That part of metaphysics which discusses the issue of whether there is a God and what God's nature is, using pure reason and no religious resources.

Naturalism: As a metaphysical position this claims that there is nothing in existence which is not included in nature. As an epistemological position this claims that there is no kind of knowledge which does not fit into the natural sciences.

Neoplatonism: A school of Hellenistic philosophy which harmonised the work of Aristotle and Plato with the emphasis on Plato. Associated with Plotinus, Proclus, Augustine, Pseudo-Dionysius, Boethius.

Noumenal: The adjective deriving from the Kantian distinction between phenomena and noumena, pertaining to objects as they are in themselves and not relative to human cognition.

Nous: The Greek word for mind. Used by Aristotle to also describe the faculty of grasping first principles of an argument, which themselves cannot be known on the basis of argument

Ockham's Razor: The methodological maxim which says that entities are not to be multiplied without necessity, which is attributed to the medieval philosopher, William of Ockham.

Omnipotence: The divine attribute which holds that God is all powerful.

Omniscience: The divine attribute which holds that God is all knowing.

Ontological Argument: An argument for the existence of God which uses purely a priori elements, devised by St Anselm.

Ontology: That part of philosophy which deals with being and what exists.

Panpsychism: In philosophy of mind, the position which claims that all things exhibit consciousness.

Pantheism: The view that God and nature are one.

Phenomenal: The adjective deriving from the Kantian distinction between phenomena and noumena, pertaining to objects relative to human cognition, not as they are in themselves.

Philosophical Theology: A branch of theology which uses philosophy to clarify and defend religious beliefs

Philosophy: The love of wisdom. An academic discipline which addresses fundamental questions about the nature of reality, knowledge, mind and value, not addressed by specific disciplines such as physics or psychology.

Phronesis: Practical reasoning. The kind of knowledge used in making moral judgements.

Physicists: Another name for the presocratic Greek philosophers who investigated nature (physis)

Platonist: A follower of Plato.

Polytheism: The view that there are many Gods.

Positivism: The view that the only adequate form of knowledge is scientific knowledge.

Postmodernism: A contemporary style of thought which denies the possibility of metaphysics, advocates pluralism, rejects tradition, celebrating irony and parody.

Premise: An assumption used in argumentation. A valid argument is one whose premises, if true, require that the conclusion also be true.

Presocratic: Referring to the philosophy which came before Socrates.

Problem of Evil: For theists, the problem of attempting to reconcile the existence of a good and all-powerful God with the existence of evil.

Process Philosophy: A philosophical movement, associated with the thought of Alfred North Whitehead, which sees nature as being essentially in process and which rejects substance-based styles of metaphysics.

Proposition: The philosophical term used for a sentence. It concerns the cognitive content of the sentence, rather than style or language. The following three sentences express the same proposition: 'It is raining', 'Il pleut', 'Tá sé ag cur baistigh'.

Rationalism: The epistemological position which holds that there is genuine metaphysical knowledge available using pure human reason. Typically referring to Descartes, Spinoza and Leibniz.

Rationality: The human capacity for using reason.

Realism: The metaphysical position which holds that reality exists independently of mind.

Reductio ad absurdem: Literally, a reduction to absurdity. A type of argument in which something one disagrees with is taken as a premise, which is then shown to lead to a contradiction and which is ultimately rejected.

Reductionism: In philosophy, this is the claim that some area under discussion is best understood by reference to another area. For example, someone might claim that mental talk is best explained by reference to brain function, that all talk of ideas and thoughts is best understood by reducing it to physical operations in the head. The advantage of reductionism is clarity, the disadvantage is the fear of leaving aside what is important.

Relativism: The claim that no single view of things is the correct one, but that there is a multiplicity of alternative, equally correct, views of e.g. reality, knowledge, truth, values.

Representationalism: A view in epistemology which holds that we do not have direct access to reality, but rather know it by means of representations, or ideas, which mediate the world to us.

Scholasticism: A term used to describe later medieval philosophy which makes extensive use of Aristotle's philosophy.

Scientism: The view which privileges scientific method and knowledge over all other kinds.

Skepticism (scepticism): In general, this is a philosophical position which denies that we have any speculative knowledge of things beyond ordinary beliefs (for example metaphysics or theology). It comes in many kinds.

Solipsism: The metaphysical position which holds that only oneself exists – all else being just a feature of one's consciousness.

Sophia: The Greek word for wisdom, knowledge of the highest things.

Sophist: Teacher of rhetoric in ancient Athens. Used as a pejorative term of one who is more interested in literary style than in truth.

Soul: The English word for the Greek word *psyche* and the Latin word *anima*. It is the principle which makes living things living. Some philosophers claim that the human soul, capable of reasoning, is immortal. Others deny that it makes sense to think of the soul as a substance, rather it is a function of the body and dies with it.

Substance: A major area of investigation for metaphysics, with many competing accounts. Philosophers speak of substance as the most fundamental kind of existing thing, distinguishing it from property.

Syllogism: A form of argument, in which two premises lead to a conclusion, for example 'All humans are mortal, Socrates is human, Socrates is mortal.' There are strict rules governing validity for syllogisms.

Techne: Greek term for the kind of knowledge required for making something.

Teleological: Pertaining to ends or purposes.

Term: The basic meaningful unit in a proposition under logical analysis. The proposition 'Socrates is Greek' consists of three terms; subject (the object under consideration) Socrates, predicate (the property attributed to the subject) Greek, and copula (the manner in which the predicate is connected to the subject, in this case affirmatively) is.

Theism: The claim that there exists a god who is an eternal, perfect creator.

Theodicy: Part of philosophy of religion which attempts to show the compatibility of the existence of God with the prevalence of evil.

Theology: A general term for the kind of reasoning which uses data from revealed religion.

Truth: A property of a proposition or a belief in which what it states to be the case actually is the case.

Universal: An abstract entity which is the meaning of a general term, such as 'goodness'. The problem of universals is the debate as to whether any such universals exist in reality.

Unmoved Mover: The Aristotelian doctrine that the source of motion in the universe is itself something which doesn't move.

Validity: A property of arguments. A valid argument is one whose structure is such that if the premises are true, then the conclusion has to be also true.

Verification Principle: The doctrine associated with logical positivism which holds that all meaningful propositions are either empirical statements or else rules of language. Its purpose was to outlaw metaphysics.

Vienna Circle: A group of scientifically oriented philosophers in the late 1920s who espoused logical positivism.

Virtue: A human disposition or habit which is a form of living well, an excellence which hovers between two opposing vices. For example the virtue of courage lies between cowardice and foolhardiness.